THREE-FINGER-CHORD UKULELE HYMNS

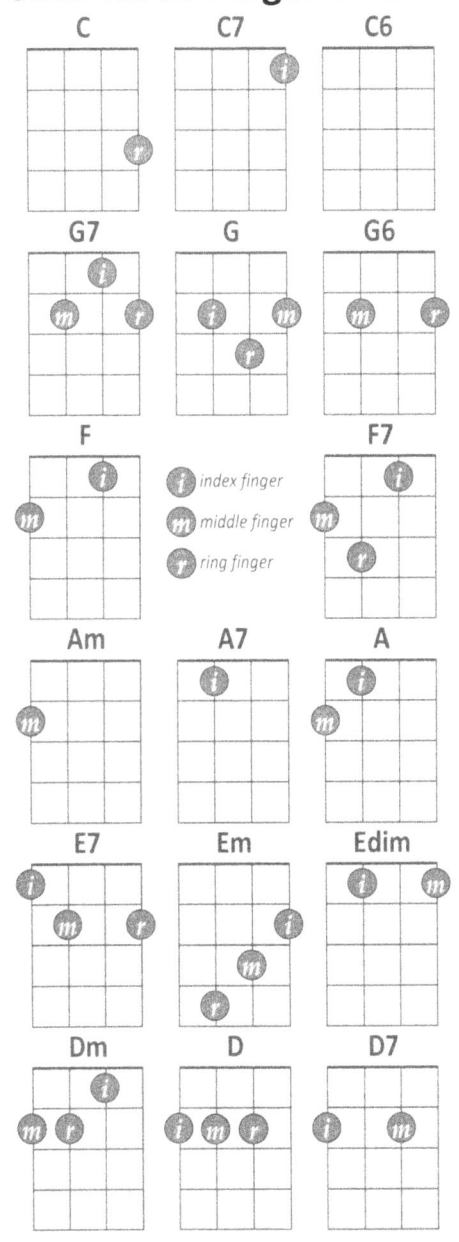

Some Three-Finger CHORDS

C, C7, C6, G7, G, G6, F, F7, Am, A7, A, E7, Em, Edim, Dm, D, D7

i index finger
m middle finger
r ring finger

Some STRUMMING Patterns

↓ down
↑ up
_ up or down without hitting strings

¾ time
↓ ↑ ↓
↓ _ ↓ ↑ ↓ _
↓ _ ↓ ↑ ↓ ↑
↓ ↑ ↓ ↑ ↓ _

⁴⁄₄ time
↓ ↑ ↓ ↑
↓ _ ↓ ↑
_ ↑ ↓ ↑
↓ ↑ _ ↑

Some 4 finger PICKING Patterns

¾ time
tr i m
tr m i
t i mr

⁴⁄₄ time
r m i t
t i m r
tr m i m

strings: 4th 3rd 2nd 1st

	G	C	E	A
4 finger picking				
down↓	*t* (thumb)			
up↑		*i* (index finger)		
up↑			*m* (middle finger)	
up↑				*r* (ring finger)

	G	C	E	A
3 finger picking				
down↓	*t* (thumb)			
down↓		*t* (thumb)		
up↑			*i* (index finger)	
up↑				*m* (middle finger)

"•" in a song means *repeat the previous chord*.
"↓" in a song calls for *one down-stroke*.
A song's **First Note** is indicated beneath the picking patterns as in "**open C**" or "**3rd fret on A**" or "**open A (low)**" meaning (an octave lower), etc.

Stephen Joseph Wolf
idjc.org/ukulele

How it happened: *A Different Kind of Twelve Steps*

1. Got an ukulele that will stay in tune ($50+).
2. Got one of those electronic tuners (<$10).
3. Learned the chords C, Am, F, and G7.
4. Played *Away In A Manger* (#18) many times.
5. Kept the ukulele next to my recliner.
6. Picked other songs and learned more chords.
7. Explored $^3_4$ time and $^4_4$ time.
8. Experimented with picking patterns.
9. "Figured out" chords on these songs.
10. Watched many ultranet videos.
11. Practiced with chord progressions.
12. Saw Jake Shimabukuro at the Ryman.

Happily Addicted?

Dear Ukulele Companion-Beginner,

The Trappist monk Thomas Merton wrote that as pray-ers we are always beginners. Don't yet know if it is true of an ukulele player, for this book is by an uke newbie. Our *Hey Deddy* Charlie Wolf used to say that everyone ought play a musical instrument. I tried learning the guitar with half of my brothers; it didn't take. Tried the cello in seminary; didn't take. Gave the piano a fair shot as a new priest; didn't take. When brothers and cousins were guitaring Christmas before last, and I spoke of old attempts at guitar, brother Danny strummed C, G, and F, and said that's all I need to learn to begin. A light came on. Gave myself an uke for Christmas, and it stared at me accusingly until the October vacation, when I learned C, G, and F, and for six months played the thing every day.

These songs (from *Hinge Hour Singer*) have been part of my daily life for twenty-five years in the *Liturgy of the Hours*, a prayer form used by Catholic priests, religious, and a growing number of lay faithful, so right away I wanted to start singing them with ukulele chords. Peppering brothers Greg and Danny last Thanksgiving about how to do this, they both said, "You'll figure it out." When Greg became annoyed, I kept asking questions until he stood to walk away as I said, "I want to know what chords to use to play *Creator of the Stars of Night*! I want to play *Creator of the Stars of Night*!" He turned and kind of yelled, "Of course you do! And who wouldn't!" Brother's button pushed. Success.

Still able to play only chords using the index, middle, and ring fingers of my left hand, that is all you will find in this book. Brother Kevin assures me the more difficult chords will come later.

So this book is by a beginner for a beginner who just wants some chords to play *Creator of the Stars of Night* and a bunch of other traditional hymn melodies. This should truly be considered only a place to begin, for you, companion-beginner, may very well want to sing in a different key, or choose a more beautiful strumming or picking pattern, or change some lyrics back to their originals, or construct some better chord progressions. Indeed, if you become convinced that in any of these songs I have made a mistake which could do harm to a beginner, please let me know through www.idjc.org/contact, for the nearest I've come to a real music education, after the 4th grade army-bean song with Steve Volz, John Varley and Randy Karl, was from Music Director Steve Janco in the Mundelein Seminary choir.

A big thank you to the brothers, cousin Karen Slater, June Esquilin (Music Director at Immaculate Conception Church), Danny Chartrand (an IC music minister and music teacher at Rossview High School), Ben Carr (who provided a surprise lesson when he came through Nashville), Mary's Music in Clarksville, Nashville Violins, friends and parish staff who have tolerated my ukulele excitement, and the IC UKES in Clarksville.

Steve Wolf

Three-Finger-Chord Ukulele Hymns
May 30, 2018

ISBN 978-1-937081-65-2   Copyright © 2018, 2023   Stephen Joseph Wolf. All rights reserved.

Song texts herein composed by Stephen J. Wolf on pages 19, 30 (& 134), 31, 33, 34, 37, 62, 74-75, 93, & 107 and verses of songs on pages 28, 72, 76, 96-97, 105, 128, & 129 appeared previously in *Hinge Hour Singer*, and may be freely treated as in the public domain.

The remaining songs herein by other authors are understood by the publisher to be in the public domain. If this is thought in error, please contact the publisher. Most of the song texts have been altered slightly, and some are marked for an alternate melody. Original texts and music tunes for most of these can be found at www.nethymnal.org,

Corrections were made to songs on pages **25, 29, 41, 49, 130,** and **135,** on **November 30, 2018,** and to songs on pages **5**, 16, **27**, 36, **56**, 57, **68**, 69, 71, **74/75, 76**, 81, **82**, 84, **85**, 88, **92**, 93, **96, 97**, 99, **102**, 107, **111, 121, 131, 141** on **August 28, 2019**.

For those who purchased earlier printings, these chord progressions can be downloaded at **idjc.org/ukulele**.

THREE-FINGER-CHORD UKULELE HYMNS

2 UKULELE STRUNG for a LEFT-HANDED PLAYER

ADVENT (13 songs)
3 Come Redeemer Of Our Race
4 Come Thou Long Expected Jesus
5 Comfort Comfort O My People
6 Creator Of The Stars Of Night
7 Faith Of Our Ancestors
8 Draw Near to Your Jerusalem, O Lord
9 The Angel Gabriel From Heaven Came
10 Immaculate Mary
11 O Come Divine Messiah
12 O Come O Come Emmanuel
14 On Jordan's Bank
15 The Advent Of Our King
16 The King Shall Come

CHRISTMAS (24 songs)
17 Angels We Have Heard On High
18 Away In A Manger
19 Gladly Magi From Of Old
20 Go Tell It On The Mountain
21 God Rest Ye Merry Gentle Folk
22 Hark A Thrilling Voice Is Sounding
23 Hark The Herald Angels Sing
24 In His Temple Come Behold Him
25 It Came Upon the Midnight Clear
26 Joy To The World
27 O Come All Ye Faithful
28 O Come Little Children
29 O Holy Night
30 O Little Town Of Bethlehem
31 Of The Father's Love Begotten
32 Rise Up Shepherd And Follow
33 Silent Night
34 The First Noel
36 The God Whom Earth And Sea And Sky
37 Virgin-Born We Bow Before You
38 Songs Of Thankfulness And Praise
39 We Three Kings Of Orient Are
40 What Child Is This
41 Lo How A Rose E'er Blooming

LENT (17 songs)
42 All Glory Laud And Honor
43 At The Name of Jesus
44 O My God My God Why   *Psalm 22*
46 Crown Him With Many Crowns
47 Forty Days And Forty Nights
48 Lord Who Throughout These Forty Days
49 O Saving Victim
50 O Sacred Head Now Wounded
51 O Sacred Head Surrounded
52 Praise To The Holiest In The Height
53 Sing My Tongue The Savior's Glory
54 Somebody's Knockin'
55 When I Survey The Wondrous Cross
56 The Glory Of These Forty Days
57 Take Up Your Cross
58 The Word Of God Proceeded Forth
59 At The Cross Her Station Keeping

EASTER (15 songs)
60 Alleluia! Sing To Jesus
61 Christ The Lord Is Ris'n Today
62 Crown Him With Many Crowns
63 Full Easter Joy The Day Was Bright
64 At The Lamb's High Feast We Sing
65 Holy Feast You Holy Day – Easter
66 Holy Feast You Holy Day – Ascension
67 Holy Feast You Holy Day – Pentecost
68 Jesus Christ Is Ris'n Today
69 Sing With All The Saints In Glory
70 The Day Of Resurrection
71 The Head That Once Was Crowned...
72 The Strife Is O'er
73 Ye Sons And Daughters
74 Come Creator Spirit

ORDINARY TIME (69 songs)
76 A Mighty Fortress Is Our God
77 Amazing Grace
78 All Creatures Of Our God And King
80 God Our Refuge   *Psalm 46*
81 As Abba Loves You   *John 15*
82 At Break Of Day   *Psalm 90*
83 Eternal Invisible God Only Wise
84 Blessed Be   *Ephesians 1*
85 Joyful Joyful We Adore You
86 Beautiful Savior   *Psalm 45:2*
87 Come Holy Spirit Whoever One
88 Comfort Comfort O My People
89 Crown Him With Many Crowns
90 Face To Face   *Psalm 82*
91 Let All Mortal Flesh Keep Silence
92 From All That Dwell Below The Skies
93 I Know That My Redeemer Lives
94 For the Beauty of the Earth
95 Great Are the Works...   *Ps 111*
96 Holy God We Praise Your Name
97 Holy Holy Holy
98 How Can I Keep from Singing
99 How Lovely Is...   *Psalm 84*
100 I Heard the Voice of Jesus Say
101 I Sing the Mighty Pow'r of God
102 In Christ There Is No East or West
103 Jerusalem My Happy Home
104 Jesus My Lord My God My All
105 Let Glory Be to God On High
106 Lord When at Your Last Supper
107 Open The Ancient...   *Psalm 24*
108 Lord Of All Being Throned Afar
109 To You We Owe...   *Psalm 65*
110 Lord Your Almighty Word (*Light*)
111 Now Thank We All Our God
112 Love Divine All Love Excelling
113 Prophets Out of Ancent Times
114 There's a Wideness in God's Mercy
115 O God Our Help in Ages Past
116 O Breathe on Me O Breath of God
117 The King of Love My Shepherd Is
118 O Lord of Life
119 On This Day the First of Days
120 Praise God From Whom All...
121 Praise My Soul the King of...
122 Praise The Lord You Heav'ns...
123 Praise to the Lord the Almighty
124 Shepherd of Souls
125 We Walk By Faith
126 The Church's One Foundation
127 Our Father All Creating
128 We Plow the Fields and Scatter
129 Of Your Singular Justice
130 Take Lord Receive
   (O God, Grant Me Serenity)
131 Blest Holy (The Beatitudes)
132 We Gather Together
133 What A Friend We Have in Jesus
134 What Wondrous Love
135 Be Still My Soul
136 Holy Mary Graceful Mother
137 Holy Joseph
138 O Sanctissima
139 On This Day O Beautiful Mother
140 Stephen Deacon Protomartyr
141 For All The Saints
142 Lord God Sabaoth El Adonai
143 Let Us Break Bread Together
144 America (My Country 'tis of Thee)
145 The Lord's Prayer

146 **CHORD PROGRESSIONS**
152 **INDEX of MELODIES**

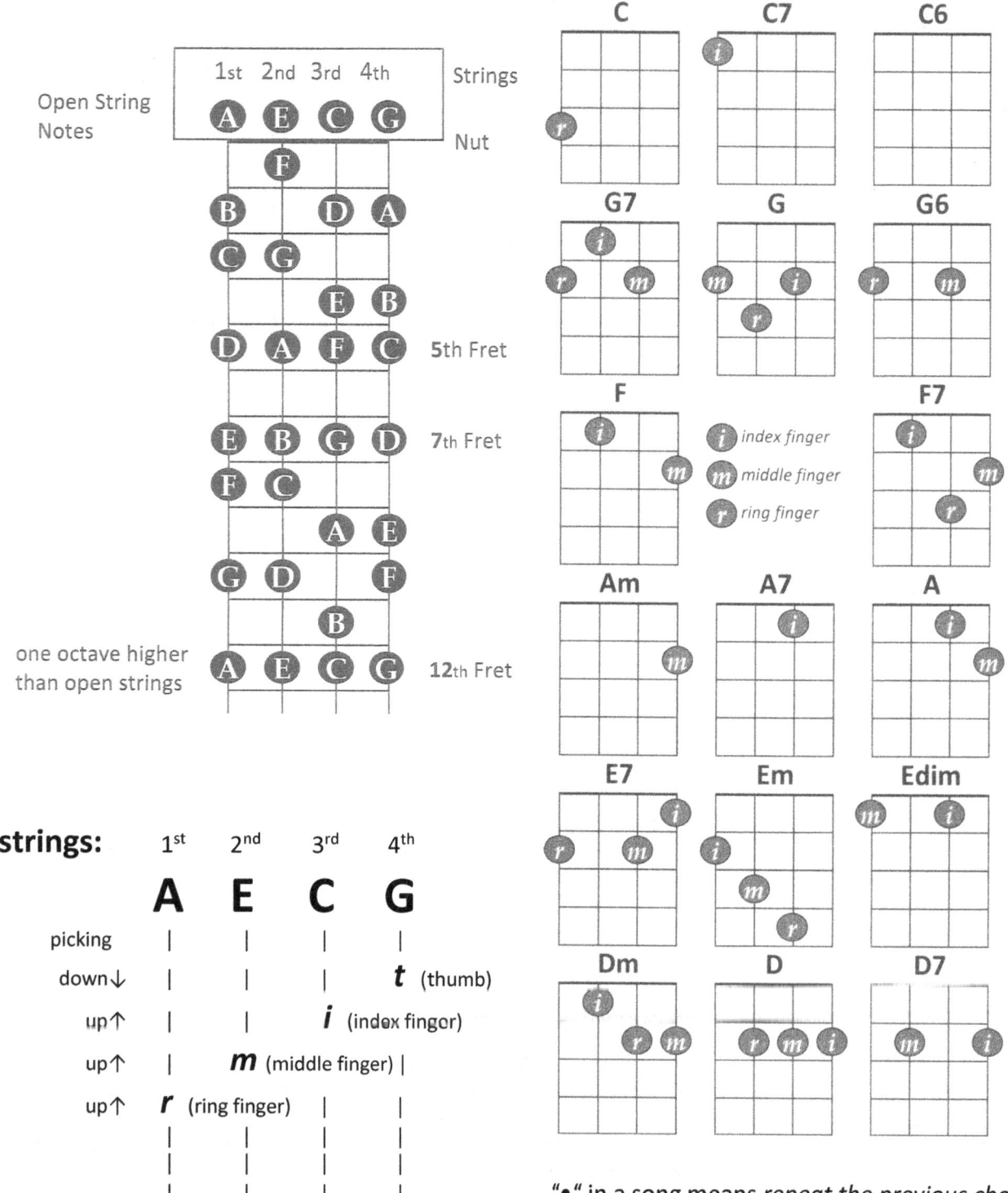

ADVENT

COME REDEEMER OF OUR RACE

C 4/4
↓ _ ↓ ↑

4 fingers *r m i t*
(see Title Page)
1st string **A** *up* with *ring finger*
2nd string **E** *up* with *middle fingr*
3rd string **C** *up* with *index finger*
4th string **G** *down* with *thumb*

Text: *Veni Redemptor gentium*, ascribed to Ambrose of Milan, d. 397,
translated by Charles Wesley, altered
Music: 7 7 7 7 HEINLEIN, Attributed to Martin Herbst, d. 1681
Popular melody for: *Forty Days and Forty Nights*, page 47

3 fingers A C E G
(see Title Page)
A string *up* with *middle*
C string *down* with *thumb*
E string *up* with *index*
G string *down* with *thumb*

3

open E (first note of the melody)

① 1

   C   **F**   **Am**   **C** • **G7**   **F**   **E7**
Come, Re-deem-er of our race, Choic-est Gift of heav'n-ly grace!
  •   **F**   **G7**   **C** • **G7**   **E7** **Am** ↓
Be the bless-ed vir-gin's Son; Join your race on earth be-gun.

② 2

   C   **F**   **Am**   **C** • **G7**   **F**   **E7**
Both of hu-man blood and birth and of God he comes to earth
  •   **F**   **G7**   **C** • **G7**   **E7** **Am** ↓
Ho-ly Spir-it breath con-ceived. God and hu-man, we be-lieve.

③ 3

   C   **F**   **Am**   **C** • **G7**   **F**   **E7**
Wond-rous, this ex-pect-ed Child Of the vir-gin un-de-filed!
  •   **F**   **G7**   **C** • **G7**   **E7** **Am** ↓
By the world he'll be dis-owned, Still to be in heav'n en-throned.

④ 4

          C   **F**   **Am**   **C**
Bright-ly will your man-ger shine!
  •   **G7**   **F**   **E7**
Glo-rious in its light div-ine:
  •   **F**   **G7**   **C**
Let our sin not cloud this light;
  •   **G7**   **E7**   **Am** ↓
Keep our gift of faith thus bright.

COME THOU LONG EXPECTED JESUS

ADVENT — HH Singer, pg 10

C 4/4
↓ _ ↓ ↑
4 tr m i m
3 A C E G
open G (low)

Text: Charles Wesley, *Hymns for the Nativity of our Lord,* 1745, altered
Music: 87 87 D, STUTTGART, Christian F. Witt, 1715;
adapted by Henry J. Gauntlett, d.1876

1

| C | Am | G7 | C | G7 | Am | G7 | C |
Come, Thou long ex-pect-ed Je-sus Born to set your peo-ple free;

| Am | G7 | F | Am | C | G7 | F | C | ↓ |
From our fears and sins re-lease us, Let us find our rest in thee.

2

| C | Am | G7 | C | G7 | Am | G7 | C |
Is-rael's strength and con-so-la-tion, Hope of all the earth you are;

| Am | G7 | F | Am | C | G7 | F | C | ↓ |
Dear de-sire of ev-'ry na-tion, Joy of ev-'ry long-ing heart.

3

| C | Am | G7 | C | G7 | Am | G7 | C |
Born your peo-ple to de-liv-er, Born a child and yet a king,

| Am | G7 | F | Am | C | G7 | F | C | ↓ |
Born to reign in us for-ev-er, Now your gra-cious king-dom bring.

4

| C | Am | G7 | C | G7 | Am | G7 | C |
By your own e-ter-nal Spir-it Rule in all our hearts a-lone;

| Am | G7 | F | Am | C | G7 | F | C | ↓ |
By your all suf-fic-ient mer-it, Raise us to your glo-rious throne.

HH Singer, pg 15   ADVENT   5

COMFORT COMFORT O MY PEOPLE

C
↓↑↓ & ↓↑↓↑
4 *tr m i* & *r m i t*
3 AG E C & A G E C
open C

Text: based on Isaiah 40:1-8 for the Feast of John the Baptist,
Johann G. Olearius, 1611-1684, trans. by Catherine Winkworth, 1827-1878, alt.
See page 88 (verse 2) for an additional verse.
Music: 87 87 77 88, GENEVA 42, Claude Goudimel, *Geneva Psalter,* 1551

1

   C   Am   F↓↑↓↑   G7↓↑↓↑ C   Am   E7↓↑↓↑ C↓↑↓↑
Com-fort, com-fort, O my peo-ple,   Speak of peace, thus says our God;
   C   Am   F↓↑↓↑   G7↓↑↓↑ C   Am   E7↓↑↓↑ C↓↑↓↑
Com-fort those who sit in dark-ness,   Mourn-ing un-der sor-row's load;
Am   G7   Am↓↑↓↑ G7↓↑↓↑ G7   Am   F↓↑↓↑   E7↓↑↓↑
Speak un-to Je-ru-sa-lem   Of the peace that waits for them;
   C   F   C↓↑↓↑   Am↓↑↓↑ Am   F   G7↓↑↓↑ C↓↑↓↑ •
Tell her all her sins I cov-er,   And that war-fare now is o-ver.

2

   C   Am   F↓↑↓↑   G7↓↑↓↑ C   Am   E7↓↑↓↑ C↓↑↓↑
For the her-ald's voice is cry-ing   In the des-ert far and near,
   C   Am   F↓↑↓↑   G7↓↑↓↑ C   Am   E7↓↑↓↑ C↓↑↓↑
Call-ing peo-ple to re-pen-tance   Since the king-dom now is here.
Am   G7   Am↓↑↓↑ G7↓↑↓↑ G7   Am   F↓↑↓↑   E7↓↑↓↑
Now that warn-ing cry o-bey!   Now pre-pare for God a way!
   C   F   C↓↑↓↑   Am↓↑↓↑ Am   F   G7↓↑↓↑ C↓↑↓↑ •
Let the val-leys rise to meet him, And the hills bow down to greet him.

3

   C   Am   F↓↑↓↑   G7↓↑↓↑
Make now straight what long was crook-ed,
   C   Am   E7↓↑↓↑ C↓↑↓↑
Make the rough-er pla-ces plain;
   C   Am   F↓↑↓↑   G7↓↑↓↑ C   Am   E7↓↑↓↑ C↓↑↓↑
Let our hearts be true and hum-ble,   As be-fits the ho-ly   reign.
Am   G7   Am↓↑↓↑ G7↓↑↓↑ G7   Am   F↓↑↓↑   E7↓↑↓↑
For the glo-ry of the Lord   O-ver earth is shed a-broad.
   C   F   C↓↑↓↑   Am↓↑↓↑ Am   F   G7↓↑↓↑ C↓↑↓↑ •
Hu-man be-ings, see the to-ken   That God's word is nev-er bro-ken.

ADVENT

CREATOR OF THE STARS OF NIGHT

3/4
↓↑↓ or ↓_↓   Text: 7th Century unknown author; translated by John M. Neale, 1852, altered
4 t r i m or t m i r m i   Music: CONDITOR, LM; *Conditor Alme Siderum*,
3 A E C A E G (3 finger roll)   Sarum plainsong, Mode IV

open E

1

```
     C    G7      F      G7           F     C    Am      E7
Cre-a-tor of the stars of night,  Your peo-ple's ev- er-last-ing light,
     F    Am    •     C     Am      G7    Am      E7  G7
Re-deem-er Je – sus, save us all, And hear your ser-vants when we call.
```

2

```
     C    G7      F      G7            F     C    Am     E7
You griev-ing that the an-cient curse Should doom to death a u-ni-verse,
     F    Am    •     C    Am      G7    Am      E7  G7
Find now the med-i-cine of grace, To save and heal the hu-man race.
```

3

```
     C    G7      F      G7
See now the Bride-groom of the bride,
     F     C    Am    E7
As drew the world to eve-ning tide;
     F    Am    •     C     Am   G7    Am      E7  G7
Pro-ceed-ing from a vir-gin shrine,  As ful-ly hu-man and div-ine.
```

4

```
     C    G7      F      G7
The Awe-some Name, ma-jes-tic now,
     F     C    Am    E7
All knees to bend and hearts to bow;
     F    Am    •     C    Am      G7    Am      E7  G7
All things ce-les-tial God does own, And things ter-res-trial, God a-lone.
```

5

```
     C    G7      F      G7         F     C    Am     E7
To God the Fa-ther, God the Son,  And God the Spir-it, Three in One,
     F    Am    •     C    Am      G7    Am      E7  G7  C
Laud, ho-nor, might, and glo-ry be From age to age e-ter-nal-ly.
```

HH Singer, pg 17 — ADVENT — 7

FAITH OF OUR ANCESTORS

3/4
↓_ ↓ ↑ ↓_
4 tr m i
3 A E C A E G

Text: Frederick W. Faber, *Jesus and Mary,* 1849; refrain by James G. Walton, 1874; altered from original *Faith of Our Fathers*
Music: ST. CATHERINE, LM; Henry F. Hemy, 1864; adapted by James G. Walton, 1874

open E

(1)
    C   Am   G7   C
Faith of our **an**-**ces**-**tors**, liv\-ing still,
    •   Am   F   G7
In spite of dun-geon, fire\ and sword;
E7   Am   G7   C
O how our hearts\ beat high\ with joy
    •   C7   G7   C
When-'er we hear that glo/-rious Word!

F   C   E7   C   •   F   G7   C ↓
Faith of our **an**-**ces**-**tors**, ho-ly faith!   We will be true to you till death.

(2)
    C   Am   G7   C
Faith of our **fa**\-**thers**, we\ will strive
    •   Am   F   G7
A-mong all peo-ples, as is our call;
E7   Am   G7   C
That through the truth\ that comes\ from God,
    •   C7   G7   C
True free-dom may be found/ by all.

F   C   E7   C   •   F   G7   C ↓
Faith of our **an**-**ces**-**tors**, ho-ly faith!   We will be true to you till death.

(3)
    C   Am   G7   C
Faith of our **mo**\-**thers**, we\ will love
    •   Am   F   G7
Both friend and foe in all\ our strife;
E7   Am   G7   C
Liv-ing and preach-ing as love\ knows how
    •   C7   G7   C
By kind-ly words and vir/-tuous life.

F   C   E7   C   •   F   G7   C ↓
Faith of our **an**-**ces**-**tors**, ho-ly faith!   We will be true to you till death.

8   ADVENT   HH Singer, pg 11

DRAW NEAR TO YOUR JERUSALEM O LORD

C 4/4
↓ ↑ _ ↑
4 r m i t
3 A C E G
open E

Text: Jeremy Taylor, *Festival and Penitential Hymns,* 1655;
abridged in *Sarum Hymnal,* 1868, altered
Music: 10 10 10 10 10 10 UNDE ET MEMORES, William H. Monk, 1823-1899
Popular melody for: *Lord Who At The First Eucharist Did Pray,* page 106

1

       C   F   Am   C   G7   •
Draw near to your Je-ru-sa-lem, O Lord,
        •   F   Am   C   E7   •
Your faith-ful peo-ple cry with one ac-cord;
      C   F   Am   C   G6   •
Ride on in tri-umph; Lord, be-hold we lay
    Am   •   G7   E7   G7   •
Our stub-born hearts and proud wills in your way!
      C   F   Am   C   G7   •
Your road is read-y and your path made straight;
       F   Am   C   G7   C   •
With long-ing ex-pec-ta-tion is our wait.

2

        •   F   Am   C   G7   •
Ho-san-na! wel-come to our hearts! For here
        •   F   Am   C   E7   •
You have a temp-le, too, as Zi-on dear;
      C   F   Am   C   G6   •
O en-ter in, dear Lord, un-bar the door;
    Am   •   G7   E7   G7   •
And in that temp-le dwell for-ev-er-more.
      C   F   Am   C   G7   •
Your road is read-y and your path made straight;
       F   Am   C   G7   C   ↓
With long-ing ex-pec-ta-tion is our wait.

THE ANGEL GABRIEL FROM HEAVEN CAME

C 4/4
↓ ↑ _ ↑
4 *r m i t*
3 A C E G
open E

Text: from *Birjina gaztettobat zegoen,* traditional Basque Carol;
translated by Sabine Baring-Gould, d.1924, altered significantly for a different melody
Music: 10 10 10 10 10 10 UNDE ET MEMORES, William H. Monk, 1823-1899
Popular melody for: *Lord Who At The First Eucharist Did Pray,* page 106

1

```
              C       F      Am     C      G7    •
         The an-gel Ga-bri-el from heav-en came,
                  •       F      Am    C      E7    •
         With wings as drift-ed snow and eyes as flame;
              C       F      Am     C      G6    •
         "All hail," the an-gel said, "O low-ly place,
              Am     •     G7     E7    G7    •
         Most high-ly fa-vored maid-en, full of grace."
 C         F      Am     C   G7 •    F      Am    C   G7  C •
Of her would come the Christ Em-man-u-el; With all the an-gels, "Glo-ri-a!" we tell.
```

2

```
                  •       F      Am    C      G7    •
         "For know a bless-ed Moth-er you shall be,
                  •       F      Am    C      E7    •
         All gen-er-a-tions' praise e-ter-nal-ly;
              C       F      Am     C      G6    •
         Your Son shall be Em-man-u-el, fore-told,
              Am     •     G7     E7    G7    •
         Most high-ly fa-vored la-dy, from of old."
 C         F      Am     C   G7 •    F      Am    C   G7  C •
Of her would come the Christ Em-man-u-el; With all the an-gels, "Glo-ri-a!" we tell.
```

3

```
                  •       F      Am    C      G7    •
         Then gen-tle Ma-ry meek-ly bowed her head;
                  •       F      Am    C      E7    •
         "To me be as it pleas-es God!" she said.
              C       F      Am     C      G6    •
         "My soul shall laud and mag-ni-fy the Name."
              Am     •     G7     E7    G7    •
         Most high-ly fa-vored la-dy, liv-ing flame.
 C         F      Am     C   G7 •    F      Am    C   G7  C •
Of her would come the Christ Em-man-u-el; With all the an-gels, "Glo-ri-a!" we tell.
```

10   ADVENT   HH Singer, pg 13

IMMACULATE MARY

³/₄
↓_ ↓↑ ↓_ or ↓↑↓
4 *tr i m*
3 A E C A E G
open G (low)
SLOWLY

Text: anonymous in *Parochial Hymn Book*; Boston, 1897; revision of *Hail Virgin,* by Jeremiah Cummings, altered
Music: 11 11 LOURDES HYMN with refrain, traditional Pyrenean Melody, pub. Grenoble, 1882; altered by Augustus Edmonds Tozer, d.1910

           C   Am   G7   C

① **Im**-**mac**-**u**-**late** Ma-ry,   your prais-es we\ sing.

     •   Am   G7   C

    You reign now in heav-en   with Je-sus our\ King.

       F   C   G7   C

     A-ve, A-ve, A-ve, Ma-ri- a!

       F   C   G7   C   ↓

     A-ve, A-ve, Ma-ri / \-a!

     •   Am   G7   C

② **In** heav-en the bless-ed   your glo-ry pro\-claim;

     •   Am   G7   C

    On earth we your chil-dren   in-voke your fair\ name.

       F   C   G7   C

     A-ve, A-ve, A-ve, Ma-ri- a!

       F   C   G7   C   ↓

     A-ve, A-ve, Ma-ri / \-a!

     •   Am   G7   C

③ **We** pray for our Mo-ther,   the Church up-on\ earth,

     •   Am   G7   C

    And bless, Ho-ly Ma-ry,   The land of our\ birth.

       F   C   G7   C

     A-ve, A-ve, A-ve, Ma-ri- a!

       F   C   G7   C   ↓

     A-ve, A-ve, Ma-ri / \-a!

ADVENT

O COME DIVINE MESSIAH

C $^6_8$
↓ ↑ ↓
4 *tr i m* or Claw A↓G
open G (low)

Text: Abbe Simon-Joseph Pellegrin, d. 1745; translated by S. Mary of St. Philip, 1877, altered
Music: 78 76 VENEZ DIVIN MESSIE, Traditional French Carol, 16th C.

①
    C   Am   F C   F   Am   C   G7
O come, div-ine Mes-si-ah; The world in si-lence waits\ the day
    C   Am   F C   Am   G7   C ↓
When hope shall sing its tri-umph And sad-ness flee\ a-way…

REFRAIN
    G7   Am   C • G7   Am   C
Dear Sav-ior haste! Come, come to earth.
    F   G7   F   G7
Dis-pel the night and show your face,
    F   G7   E7   G7 ↓
And bid us hail the dawn of grace…

②
    C   Am   F C
O Christ, whom na-tions sigh for,
    F   Am   C   G7
Whom priest and proph-et long\ fore-told,
    C   Am   F C
Come, break the cap-tive fet-ters,
    Am   G7   C ↓
Re-deem the long\-lost fold…   REFRAIN

③
    C   Am   F C
You come in peace and meek-ness
    F   Am   C   G7
And low-ly will your cra\-dle be;
    C   Am   F C
All clothed in hu-man weak-ness
    Am   G7   C ↓
Shall we your God\-head see.   REFRAIN

④ *(Repeat First Verse without the refrain.)*

12   ADVENT   HH Singer, pg 7

O COME O COME EMMANUEL

4/4

↓↑_↑ ↓↑_↑   Text: From the late Advent "O Antiphons" used with the Canticle of Mary, 12th century;
4 tr m i m tr m i m   translated by John M. Neale, 1851, altered
3 A C E G A C E G   Music: VENI EMMANUEL, LM with refrain; 15th C.; adapt. by Thomas Helmore, 1856

open A (low)
    Am   **G7**   **Am**   **C**   **G7**   **Am**

① **O come, O come,** Em-man/\-u-el, And ran-som cap-tive Is\\-ra-el,

    F   **C**   **G7**   **Am**   **G7**   **Am**

That mourns in lone-ly ex\-ile here   Un-til the Son of God/\ ap-pear.

G7   **Am**   **G7**   **Am**   **C**   **E7**   **Am** ↓

<u>**RE-JOICE! RE-JOICE!**</u> Em-man /\ -u-el   Shall come to you, O Is \\ -ra-el.

Dec 17   •   **G7**   **Am**

②   **O come now Wis-dom** of our God Most High,

         C   **G7**   **Am**

With love and ten-der strength, Cre-a-tor Guide;

         F   **C**   **G7**

To us the path of true know-ledge show,

         Am   **G7**   **Am**

And teach us in her sa-ving Way to go.   *Re-joice!...*

Dec 18   •   **G7**   **Am**

③   **O come great Lord** of an-cient Is-ra-el,

         C   **G7**   **Am**

Who in the fire to Mos-es showed your-self,

         F   **C**   **G7**

And gave the Law up-on Si-nai height;

         Am   **G7**   **Am**

Stretch out your hand and free us by your might.   *Re-joice!...*

Dec 19   •   **G7**   **Am**

④   **O come raise up,** deep Root of Jes-se's tree,

         C   **G7**   **Am**

A sign for peo-ple seek-ing to be free,

         F   **C**   **G7**

Be-fore whom na-tions' rul-ers will bow,

         Am   **G7**   **Am**

Come save with-out de-lay to keep your vow.   *Re-joice!...*

13

| G7   Am   G7   Am   C   E7   Am ↓
RE-JOICE! RE-JOICE! Em-man /\ -u-el Shall come to you, O Is \\ -ra-el.

Dec 20
⑤
     •   G7   Am
  O come, **O Key** of Da-vid, Roy-al Pow'r,
    C   G7   Am
  And o-pen gates to end our cap-tive hour;
    F   C   G7
  For all be-hind a dark pris-on wall
    Am   G7   Am
  Re-move the fear that blocks your sac-red call. *Re-joice!...*

Dec 21
⑥
     •   G7   Am
  O come, **O Ra-diant Dawn**, e-ter-nal light,
    C   G7   Am
  Come shine and put the fear of death to flight.
    F   C   G7
  In splen-dor o-ver dwell-ings of shade
    Am   G7   Am
  The sun of Jus-tice has our full debt paid. *Re-joice!...*

Dec 22
⑦
     •   G7   Am
  O come, **O King** of na-tions, migh-ty arc,
    C   G7   Am
  Au-then-tic joy of ev-'ry hu-man heart;
    F   C   G7
  O Key-stone, true foun-da-tion to trust,
    Am   G7   Am
  Come save us whom you fash-ion from the dust. *Re-joice!...*

Dec 23
⑧
     •   G7   Am
  O come, **de-sire** of all the na-tions, bind
    C   G7   Am
  In one the hearts and souls of hu-man-kind;
    F   C   G7
  Come make our sad di-vis-ions to cease,
    Am   G7   Am
  And be, Em-man-u-el, our King of Peace. *Re-joice!...*

14   ADVENT   HH Singer, pg 9

ON JORDAN's BANK

Text: Charles Coffin, d.1749; translated by John Chandler, d.1876, altered
Music: WINCHESTER NEW, CM, *Musikalisches Handbuch,* Hamburg, 1690;
adapted by William H. Havergal, d.1870

C 4/4
↓ ↑ _ ↑
4 *tr m i m*
3 A C E G
open C

**① **
     F   Dm   C   Am
On Jor-dan's bank the Bap-tist's cry
     C7   G7   C   •
An-nounc-es that the Lord is nigh;
     F   Dm   C7   G7
A-wake and heark-en, for he brings
     F   C   F   •
Glad ti-dings of the King of kings.

**② **
     •   Dm   C   Am
Then cleansed be ev-'ry soul from sin;
     C7   G7   C   •
Make straight the way of God with-in,
     F   Dm   C7   G7
Pre-pare we in our hearts a home,
     F   C   F   •
Where such a migh-ty guest may come.

**③ **
     •   Dm   C   Am
For you are our sal-va-tion, Lord,
     C7   G7   C   •
Our ref-uge and our sure re-ward;
     F   Dm   C7   G7
Shine forth, and let your light re-store
     F   C   F   •
Our souls to heav'n-ly grace once more.

**④ **
     •   Dm   C   Am   C7   G7   C   •
All praise, e-ter-nal Son, to thee   Whose ad-vent set your peo-ple free,
     F   Dm   C7   G7   F   C   F   •
Whom with the Fa-ther we a-dore   And Ho-ly Spir-it ev-er-more.

THE ADVENT OF OUR KING

Text: Charles Coffin, d.1749; translated by Robert Campbell, d.1868, altered
Music: 66 86 ST. THOMAS (WILLIAMS); Aaron Williams, d.1776

C
↓ ↑ _ ↑
4 *tr m i m*
3 A C E G
open G (low)

**① **

```
     C       Am     G7 ↓      C             F     G7 ↓
The ad-vent of our\ King  Our/ thoughts must\ now em-ploy;
     C       G7      C       G7         F     G7     C ↓
Then let us meet him on/ the/ road  With songs of\ ho-ly joy.
```

**② **

```
          Am     G7 ↓     C          F     G7 ↓
The co-e-ter-nal\ Son  A/ maid-en's\ off-spring see;
     C       G7     C      G7        F     G7     C ↓
A ser-vant's form Christ did/ put/ on,  To set his\ peo-ple free.
```

**③ **

```
          Am     G7 ↓     C           F     G7 ↓
In glo-ry from his\ throne  A/-gain will\ Christ de-scend,
     C       G7       C      G7        F     G7     C ↓
And sum-mon all who are/ his/ own  To joys that\ nev-er end.
```

**④ **

```
          Am       G7 ↓    C          F     G7 ↓
Our joy-ful prais-es\ sing  To/ Christ, who\ set us free;
     C       G7       C       G7        F     G7     C ↓
As trib-ute to the Fa/-ther/ bring,  And Ho-ly\ Ghost, to thee.
```

16   ADVENT   HH Singer, pg 14

THE KING SHALL COME

4/4
↓ ↑ _ ↑
4 r m i t
3 A C E G
open C

Text: author unknown; translated from Greek by John Brownlie,
Hymns of the Russian Church, 1907
Music: MCKEE, CM; African American Spiritual, arranged by Harry T. Burleigh, 1866-1949
Popular melody for: *In Christ There Is No East or West*, page 102

1

```
         C           G7           C7         F
The/ King shall come when/ morn-ing dawns,
       Am        F          C          Am
And light tri-umph\-ant/ breaks;
           E7         C          G6        C
When/ beau-ty gilds the east-ern hills,
           E7        G7         C         G7↓
And/ life/ to joy\ a-wakes.
```

2

```
         C           G7           C7         F
O/ bright-er than that/ glo-rious morn
       Am        F          C          Am
Shall this fair morn\-ing/ be,
           E7         C          G6        C
When/ Christ, our King, in beau-ty comes,
           E7        G7         C         G7↓
And/ we/ his face\ shall see.
```

3

```
         C           G7           C7         F
The/ King shall come when/ morn-ing dawns,
       Am        F          C          Am
And light and beau\-ty/ brings:
           E7         C          G6        C
Hail/, Christ the Lord! your peo-ple pray,
           E7        G7         C         •
Come/ quick/-ly, King\ of kings.
```

HH Singer, pg 23   CHRISTMAS

ANGELS WE HAVE HEARD ON HIGH

Text: French, 18th C.; translated from *Crown of Jesus Music, II,* London, 1862.
Music: 77 77 GLORIA with refrain, traditional French carol

C 4/4
↓ ↑ ↓ ↑
4 *r m i t*
3 A C E G
open E

1
    C   Am   G7   Am
An-gels we have heard on high
    C   Am   G6   C
Sweet-ly sing-ing o'er the plains,
  •   Am   G7   Am
And the moun-tains in re-ply
    C   Am   G6   C
E-cho back their joy-ous strains.

REFRAIN
  •   Am   F G7   C F   G7 G6 C   Am   C G7
Glo /\\\ / /\\\ / /\\\ /-ri-a in ex-cel-sis De-o!
   C   Am   F G7   C F   G7 G6 C   Am   C G7 C •
Glo /\\\ / /\\\ / /\\\ /-ri-a in ex-cel-sis De \ - o!

2
  •   Am   G7   Am
Shep-herds why this ju-bi-lee?
    C   Am   G6   C
Why your joy-ous strains pro-long?
  •   Am   G7   Am
Say what may the ti-dings be
    C   Am   G6   C
Which in-spire your heav'n-ly song.   **REFRAIN**

3
  •   Am   G7   Am
Come to Beth-le-hem and see
    C   Am   G6   C
Him whose birth the an-gels sing;
  •   Am   G7   Am
Come, a-dore on bend-ed knee
    C   Am   G6   C
Christ the Lord the new-born King.   **REFRAIN**

18   CHRISTMAS   HH Singer, pg. 45

AWAY IN A MANGER

$\frac{3}{4}$

↓_ ↓↑ ↓_
4   *m r i t*
  or   *t m i r m i*
3   A E C A E G
   (*3 finger roll*)

open G

Text: verses 1-2, Anon., *Little Children's Book for Schools and Families*, ca.1885;
verse 3, John T. McFarland, d. 1913, Gabriel's *Vineyard Songs*, 1892, altered
Music: 11 11 11 11 MUELLER, attributed to James R. Murray, d. 1905

1

    C   Am   F   C
A-**way** in a man-ger, no crib for a bed,
    G7   •   C   Am
The lit-tle Lord Je-sus laid down his sweet head.
    C   Am   F   C
The stars in the sky\ looked down where he lay,
    G7   C   G7   C   ↓
The lit-tle Lord Je-sus, a-sleep in the hay.

2

     •   Am   F   C
The cat-tle are low-ing, the Ba-by a-wakes,
    G7   •   C   Am
But lit-tle Lord Je-sus, no cry-ing he makes;
    C   Am   F   C
I love you, Lord Je-sus, look down from the sky
    G7   C   G7   C   ↓
And stay by my cra-dle till morn-ing is nigh.

3

     •   Am   F   C
Be near me, Lord Je-sus, I ask you to stay
    G7   •   C   Am
Close by me for-ev-er, and love me, I pray;
    C   Am   F   C
Bless all the dear chil-dren in your ten-der care,
    G7   C   G7   C   ↓
And fit us for heav-en to live with you there.

HH Singer, pg 53 — CHRISTMAS — 19

GLADLY MAGI FROM OF OLD

C 4/4
↓ _ ↓ ↑
4 tr m i m
3 A C E G
open C

Text: from Matthew 2:1-11, William C. Dix, *As With Gladness Men of Old,* 1860, altered
Music: 77 77 77 DIX, Konrad Kocher, 1838
Popular melody for: *For The Beauty Of The Earth*, page 94

1

    C   G7   F   C   Am   F   G7   C
Glad-ly / ma-gi from of old Did the guid-ing star be-hold;
 •   G7   F   C
And with / joy they hailed its light,
 Am   F   G7   C
Lead-ing on-ward, beam-ing bright,
 •   Am   G7   C
So, most gra-cious Lord, may we
 Am   F   G6   C •
Ev-er-more your glo-ry see!

2

 •   G7   F   C   Am   F   G7   C
As with / joy-ful steps they sped, Sa-vior, to your hum-ble bed,
 •   G7   F   C
There to / bend the knee be-fore
 Am   F   G7   C
You whom heav'n and earth a-dore,
 •   Am   G7   C   Am   F   G6   C •
So may we with will-ing feet Ev-er seek your mer-cy seat!

3

 •   G7   F   C   Am   F   G7   C
Ma-gi / of-fered gifts most rare At your cra-dle, crude and bare,
 •   G7   F   C   Am   F   G7   C
So may / we with ho-ly joy, Pure and free from sin's al-loy,
 •   Am   G7   C   Am   F   G6   C •
All our cost-liest trea-sures bring, Christ, to you, our heav'n-ly King!

GO TELL IT ON THE MOUNTAIN

20   CHRISTMAS   HH Singer, pg 51

C $^2_2$
↓↑↓↑
4 tr m i m
3 A C E G
open C

Text: John W. Work, Jr., 1872-1925;
Folk Songs of the American Negro, Nashville, 190
Music: 76 76 with refrain; African American Spiritual

1)
      C   •   •   •
While shep-herds kept their watch-ing
      G7   •   **C**   •
O'er si-lent flocks by night
   •   •   •   •
Be-hold through-out the heav-ens
      Dm   •   **G7** ↓
There shone a ho-ly light /.

REFRAIN_____

C   •   •   •   **G7**   •   **C**   **F**
Go, tell it on the moun-tain, O-ver the hills and ev-'ry-where\
C   •   •   •   **Am**   **G7**   **C**   ↓
Go, tell it on the moun-tain, That Je-sus Christ\ is born.

---

2)
   •   •   •   •
The shep-herds feared and trem-bled,
      G7   •   **C**   •
When lo! a-bove the earth,
   •   •   •   •
Rang out the an-gels chor-us
      Dm   •   **G7** ↓
That hailed the Sav-ior's birth /.   **REFRAIN**

3)
   •   •   •   •   **G7**   •   **C**   •
Down in a low-ly man-ger The hum-ble Christ was born
   •   •   •   •   **Dm**   •   **G7** ↓
And God sent us sal-va-tion That bless-ed Christ-mas morn/.

                                                                  REFRAIN

GOD REST YE MERRY GENTLE FOLK

C 2/2
↓↑↓↑
4 *tr m i m*
3 A C E G
open A (low)

Text: traditional English Carol, 18th C., altered
Music: 86 86 86 with refrain GOD REST YOU MERRY, *Little Book of Christmas Carols,* 1846

①

```
        Am      C    F   Am      •           F        C   •
God rest ye mer-ry, gen-tle FOLK,  let noth-ing you dis-may,
        Am      C    F   Am      •           F        C   •
Re-mem-ber Christ our Sa\-vior    was born on Christ-mas day;
    F         C        G7       C         Am     G7       E7
To save us from the e-vil pow'r  when we had gone a-stray.
```

REFRAIN

```
       F   C   F        E7   •        Am      C            G7
       O/ ti-dings of com\-fort and joy,  com-fort and joy;
       F   C   G7       E7   •        Am   •  ↓
       O/ ti/-dings of com\-fort and joy.
```

↓ with thumb; <u>slower</u>

②

```
             •          F       Am                C
        From God our heav'n-ly Fa\-ther  a bless-ed an-gel came;
        Am            F             Am                   C
        And un-to cer-tain shep\-herds   brought  ti-dings of the same;
            F           G7                  Am             E7
        How that in Beth-le-hem was born  the Son of God by name
```

                                                                REFRAIN

↓↑

③

```
             •    C    F   Am      •           F        C   •
        "So, have no fear," the an-gel said, "but find the vir-gin maid.
        Am      C    F   Am      •           F        C   •
        Of her is born the Sa\-vior,  so do not be a-fraid.
            F         C        G7       C         Am     G7       E7
        Now free are all who trus-ted their re-demp-tion would be paid"
```

                                                                REFRAIN

HARK A THRILLING VOICE IS SOUNDING

22 — CHRISTMAS — HH Singer, pg 40

C 4/4
↓ ↑ _ ↑
4 r m i t
3 A G E C
open E

Text: see Romans 13:11; unknown author, c. 900;
translated by Edward Caswall, 1849, altered
Music: 87 87 D, PLEADING SAVIOR, Joshua Leavitt, *Christian Lyre*, 1830
Popular melody for: *Sing of Mary, Pure and Lowly*

1

| C | F | C | G6 | C | F | G6 | C |

Hark, a\ thrill-ing/ voice is sound-ing! "Christ is\ nigh!" we/ hear it say;

• F C G6 C F G6 C

"Cast a\-way the/ works of dark-ness, O ye\ chil-dren/ of the day."

G6 G7 F Am G6 G7 F G7

Star-tled\ at the sol-emn\ warn-ing, Let the\ earth-bound soul a\-rise;

C F C Am C F E7 C

Christ, her\ Sun, all/ sloth dis-pel-ling, Shines up\-on the/ morn-ing skies.

2

• F C G6 C F G6 C

Lo, the\ Lamb, so/ long ex-pect-ed, Comes with\ par-don/ from a-bove.

• F C G6 C F G6 C

Let us\ haste to ap-proach his mer-cy Draw-ing\ near with/ words of love.

G6 G7 F Am G6 G7 F G7

Hon-or\, glo-ry, might, do\-min-ion, To the\ Fa-ther and the\ Son,

C F C Am C F E7 C

With the\ e-ver/-last-ing Spir-it, While e\-ter-nal/ a-ges run!

HH Singer, pg 25 CHRISTMAS 23

HARK THE HERALD ANGELS SING

C 4/4
↓↑↓↑
4 *tr m i m* 3 A C E G
open G (low)

Text: see Luke 2:14; Charles Wesley, 1739
Music: 7777777777 MENDELSSOHN, Felix Mendelssohn, 1840

**① **

```
  C          F        C       Am      G7     •     E7         C
Hark! the her-ald an-gels sing\,  "Glo-ry to the new-born King;
  •          F        C       Am      G7      F     G7        •
Peace on earth and mer-cy mild\,  God and sin-ners re-con-ciled!"
  C     •     F       Am       C     •        F       Am
Joy-ful, all ye na-tions rise\,  Join the tri-umph of the skies\;
  F     •↓↑ C↓↑ F↓↑ Am↓↑  F    G7          C        F      C
With th'an-gel-ic host pro- claim.  "Christ is/ born in Beth-le-hem!"
```

REFRAIN
```
  F     •↓↑ C↓↑ F↓↑ Am↓↑  F    G7          C         F       C  ↓
Hark! the her-ald an-gels sing, "Glo-ry/ to the new-born King!"
```

**② **

```
  •          F        C       Am      G7     •     E7         C
Christ, by high-est heav'n a-dored\.  Christ, the ev-er-last-ing Lord,
  •          F        C       Am      G7      F     G7        •
Late in time be-hold him come\,  Off-spring of the vir-gin's womb.
  C     •     F       Am       C     •        F       Am
Veiled in flesh the God-head see\,  Hail th'in-car-nate De-i-ty\!
  F     •↓↑ C↓↑ F↓↑ Am↓↑  F    G7          C        F      C
Pleased as man with us  to dwell Je-sus/, our Em-man-u-el!  REFRAIN
```

**③ **

```
  •          F        C       Am      G7     •     E7         C
Come, De-sire of na-tions, come\,  Fix in us your hum-ble home;
  •          F        C       Am      G7      F     G7        •
Oh, to all your-self im-part\,  Formed in each be-liev-ing heart!
  C     •     F       Am       C     •        F       Am
Hail, the heav'n-ly Prince of Peace\! Hail, the Sun of Right-eous-ness\!
  F     •↓↑ C↓↑ F↓↑ Am↓↑  F    G7          C        F      C
Light and life to  all  he  brings, Ris-en with heal-ing in his wings. REF
```

24   CHRISTMAS   HH Singer, pg 43

IN HIS TEMPLE COME BEHOLD HIM

C 4/4
↓ _ ↓ ↑
4 r m i t
3 A C E G
open C

Text: based on Luke 2:22, the Presentation of the Lord;
Henry J. Pye, d.1903, and William Cooke, d.1894, altered
Music: 87 87 87 ST. THOMAS (TANTUM ERGO), John F. Wade, d.1786
Popular melody for: *Down In Adoration Falling*, see page 53

1

```
    C       Am      F       Dm          C
In his tem-ple come be-hold him,
    Am      Dm      G7          C
See the long ex-pect-ed Lord;
    •       •       F       Dm          C
An-cient proph-ets had fore-told him;
    Am      C       Am          G7
God has now ful-filled this word,
    •       C       G7      Dm      C
Now, to praise him, Al-le-lu-ia!
    F       Dm      G7      C    ↓
Break we forth with one ac-cord.
```

2

```
    C       Am      F       Dm      C Am        Dm      G7      C
See him in the arms of Sim-eon,   Hear the grate-ful An-na's cry;
    •       •       F       Dm      C Am        C       Am      G7
While these a-ged saints a-dore him,  See him with the vir-gin lie.
    •   C   G7  Dm  C F         Dm          G7      C    ↓
Al-le-lu-ia! Al-le-lu-ia!   Lo, th'in-car-nate God Most High.
```

3

```
    C       Am      F       Dm      C Am        Dm      G7      C
Je-sus, who in pres-en-ta-tion   Bless-ings giv-en by your poor,
    •       •       F       Dm      C Am        C       Am      G7
Prince and au-thor of sal-va-tion,  Seal us with your prom-ise sure,
    •   C   G7  Dm  C F         Dm          G7      C    ↓
And pre-sent us in the Spir-it   To your Fa-ther cleansed and pure.
```

IT CAME UPON THE MIDNIGHT CLEAR

Text: Edmund H. Sears, 1849
Music: CAROL CMD, Richard S. Willis, 1850

6/8
↓_ ↓↑ ↓_
4 *tr i m*
3 A E C A E G

open G (low)

**① **

    C   F   C   •   F   Am   G7 •
It came up-on\ the mid-night clear, That glo/-rious song/ of old,
    C   F   C   •   F   G7   C •
From an-gels bend\-ing near the earth, To touch their harps\ of gold;
   E7   •   Am   C
"Peace on the earth/, good will to all,
   F   Dm   G7 •
From heav-en's all gra/-cious King."
   C   F   C •   F   G7   C ↓
The world in sol\-emn still-ness lay, To hear the an\-gels sing.

**② **

  •   F   C •   F   Am   G7•
To you, be-neath\ life's crush-ing load, Whose forms/ are bend/-ing low,
   C   F   C •   F   G7   C •
Who toil a-long\ the climb-ing way With pain-ful steps\ and slow,
   E7 •   Am   C   F   Dm   G7 •
Look now! for glad/ and gol-den hours Come swift\-ly on/ the wing.
   C   F   C •   F   G7   C ↓
O rest be-side\ the wea-ry road, And hear the an\-gels sing.

**③ **

  •   F   C •   F   Am   G7 •
For lo! the days\ are hast'n-ing on, By pro-phet-bards/ fore-told,
   C   F   C •   F   G7   C •
When with the e\-ver circ-ling years Come round the age of gold;
   E7 •   Am   C   F   Dm   G7 •
When peace shall o /-ver all the earth Its an\-cient splen/-dors fling,
   C   F   C •   F   G7   C ↓
And all the world\ send back the song Which now the an\-gels sing.

26 CHRISTMAS HH Singer, pg 49

²⁄₄

↓ ↑ ↓ ↑

4 *tr m i m*   3 A C E G

3rd fret A

JOY TO THE WORLD

Text: based on Luke 2:10 and Psalm 98; Isaac Watts, 1719, altered
Music: ANTIOCH CM, George Frideric Handel, 1742

①

```
C   F      C  •  G7 •  C •    F •  G7 •   C •••
```
Joy to the world, the Lord is come! Let earth re-ceive her King;
```
    F   •   C  •      F    •   C   •
```
Let ev\-'ry\ heart\\ pre-pare\ him\ room\\
```
    •       •       G7 •  Dm       •       F •
```
And heav'n and na-ture/ sing. And\ heav'n and na-ture/ sing.
```
    C   •       •   •      G7 •    C •
```
And\ hea/v'n, and hea \\v'n and na-ture sing.

②

```
  •  F      C  •  G7 •  C •   F •  G7 •   C •••
```
Joy to the earth, the Sa-vior reigns! Let us their songs em-ploy,
```
    F   •   C  •      F    •   C   •
```
While fields\ and\ floods\\, rocks, hills\, and\ plains\\
```
    •       •       G7 •  Dm       •       F •
```
Re-peat the sound-ing/ joy. Re\-peat the sound-ing/ joy.
```
    C   •       •   •      G7 •    C •
```
Re\-peat/, Re-peat\\ the sound-ing joy.

③

```
      •  F    C  •   G7 •   C  •
```
He rules the world with truth and grace
```
        F   •  G7 •     C    •••
```
And makes the na -tions prove
```
      F  •  C •     F  •   C  •
```
The glo\-ries\ of\\ his right\-eous\-ness\\
```
        •       •      G7    •
```
And won-ders of his/ love.
```
        Dm          •    F   •
```
And\ won-ders of his/ love.
```
      C   •       •   •     G7 •  C    ↓
```
And\ won/ -ders, won\\-ders of his love.

O COME ALL YE FAITHFUL

Text: John f. Wade, 1743; translated by Frederick Oakeley, 1841
Music: ADESTE FIDELES, attributed variously to John Wade, John Reading, or Simon Portogallo

4/4
↓ ↑ ↓ ↑
4 r m i t
3 A C E G

open C

1

```
     C    •       G7  •   E7       •      C   G7
O come, all ye faith-ful, joy-ful and tri-um-phant,
     F     G7      F    G7      E7 Am    G7   •
O come ye, O come/ ye, to Beth\-le-hem.
     C    •    Am   C   G7        C    G7   •
Come and be-hold him, born the King of an\-gels;
```

REFRAIN
```
         C         G7    ↓↑ C    •
     O come, let us a-dore him,
         E7        Am    ↓↑ C   G7
     O come, let us a-dore him,
         C         G7    ↓↑ E7  C↓↑ F  •   C  G7    C    ↓
     O come, let us a-dore him /,    Christ\ the Lord.
```

2

```
  •    •       G7  •   E7     •       C   G7
Sing, choirs of an-gels, sing in ex-ul-ta-tion;
    F    G7      F    G7    E7 Am    G7    •
O sing, all ye cit-i-zens of heav'n\ a-bove!
  C  •   Am   C  G7    C       G7    •
Glo-ry to God, all glo-ry in the high\-est;         REFRAIN
```

3

```
  •    •       G7  •    E7      •        C   G7
Yea, Lord, we greet thee, born this hap-py morn-ing;
    F    G7      F    G7   E7 Am    G7     •
O Je-sus, to thee/ be/ glo \-ry giv'n;
  C  •   Am   C  G7    C       G7    •
Word of the Fa-ther, now in flesh ap-pear\-ing.     REFRAIN
```

28   CHRISTMAS   HH Singer, pg 48

O COME LITTLE CHILDREN

4/4
↓ _ ↓ ↑
4 r m i t r m i t
3 A C E G A C E G
open G

Text: Johann C. von Schmid, d.1854; translated by Melanie Schute, d.1922, altered
Music: 11 11 11 11 IHR KINDERLEIN KOMMET, by Johann A. Schulz, d.1800

**① **

   C   •   **G7**   **C**
O come, lit-tle chil-dren; come one and come all,
    •   **Am**   **G7**   **C**
O come to the man-ger in Beth-le-hem's stall,
    G7   •   **C**   **F**
And see what our Fa-ther in heav-en a-bove
    C   **Am**   **G7**   **C**   •
Has sent to us all on this earth with his love.

**② **

    •   •   **G7**   **C**
O see, in the man-ger so meek and so mild,
    •   **Am**   **G7**   **C**
O see in the soft light the heav-en-ly child,
    G7   •   **C**   **F**
In swad-dling clothes fold-ed, his beau-ty more sweet
    C   **Am**   **G7**   **C**   •
Than an-gels, whose voic-es his low-ly birth greet.

**③ **

    •   •   **G7**   **C**
His bed, lit-tle chil-dren, a man-ger with hay;
    •   **Am**   **G7**   **C**
His Moth-er and Jo-seph in ec-sta-sy pray,
    G7   •   **C**   **F**
The shep-herds in won-der their glad wor-ship bring,
    C   **Am**   **G7**   **C**
While cho-rus of an-gels sweet Glo-ri-a's sing.

HH Singer, pg 27   CHRISTMAS

O HOLY NIGHT

6/8
↓ ↑ ↓

open E

Text: Placide Cappeau, 1847; translated from French by John S. Dwight, d. 1893, altered
Music: 11 10 11 10 11 10 11 10 10, Adolphe C. Adam, d. 1856
Said to have been the first music broadcast by radio.

①
```
     C   •      G7  •     F     •      C  G7
     O ho-ly night, the stars are bright-ly shi-ning;
     C   •   •      G7  F     C     •
     It is the night of the dear Sa-vior's birth!
         •   •   G7  •    F    •      C  G7
     Long lay the world in sin and err-or pi-ning
           •    E7   •      G7    F      E7  •  •
     Till he ap-peared and the soul felt its worth_.
     G7  •  •  •            F    C    Am G7
     A thrill of hope, the wea-ry soul re-joic-es,
        •  F   G7 •   F        C      G7    •
     For yon-der breaks a new and glo-rious morn.
     Am • •  E7       •  • G7  Dm • •      Am  •  •  •
     Fall__ on your knees__,   O hear__ the an-gel voi_-ces!
           C •G7•  F  • •   •   C  • G7       F       C  • • •
     O night_ \ div-ine__,  O\ night_   when Christ was born_!
        G7 • •    C   E7↓ x x x    •    G7      C      ↓
     O night_,  O ho-ly night\\\,     O night div-ine!
```

②
```
     C   •      G7  •     F     •      C  G7
     Tru-ly he taught us to love one an-oth-er;
     C   •   •      G7  F     C     •
     His law is love and his Gos-pel is peace.
         •   •   G7  •    F    •      C  G7
     Chains shall he break for the slave is our broth-er
           •    E7   •      G7    F      E7  •  •
     And in his Name all op-pres-sion shall cease_.
     G7  •  •  •            F    C    Am G7
     The King of kings  lay thus in hum-ble man-ger,
        •  F   G7 •   F        C      G7    •
     In all our tri-als born to be our Friend!
     Am • •  E7       •  • G7  Dm • •      Am  •  •  •
     He __ knows our need__,   to our weak_ -ness is no stran_-ger.
           C •G7•  F  • •   •   C  • G7       F       C  • • •
     Be-hold_ \ your King__;  Son of Ma_  -ry, Son of God_!
        G7 • •    C   E7↓ x  x  x    •    G7      C      ↓
     Give glo_-ry to God_: Fa - ther and Son   and Spir-it blest!
```

O LITTLE TOWN OF BETHLEHEM

30   CHRISTMAS   HH Singer, pg 44

C 4/4
↓ _ ↓ ↑
4 *tr m i m*   3 A C E G
open E

Text: based on Micah 5:2; Phillips Brooks, 1868, altered
Music: 86 86 76 86 ST.LOUIS, Lewis Henry Redner, 1868

1

| C • | G7 | F | C | G7 | E7 • |
O lit-tle town of Beth-le-hem,   How still we/ see you lie!

| • Am | G7 | F | C | E7 | C • |
A-bove a deep and dream-less sleep   The si-lent/ stars go by;

| Am | E7 | G7 • | F | Am | E7 | G7 |
Yet in your dark-ness shi-ning   The ev-er-last-ing Light;

| C | Am | G7 | F | G7 | E7 | C ↓ |
The hopes and fears of all the years Are met in you to-night.

2

| • • | G7 | F | C | G7 | E7 • |
For Christ is born of Ma\-ry,   And fa-thered/ all a-bove,

| • Am | G7 | F |
While hu-mans sleep, the an-gels keep

| C | E7 | C • |
Their watch of/ won-d'ring love.

| Am | E7 | G7 • | F | Am | E7 • |
O morn-ing stars, to-geth-er   Pro-claim the ho-ly birth

| C | Am | G7 | F | G7 | E7 | C ↓ |
And prais-es sing to God, the King, And peace to all on earth.

3

| • • | G7 | F | C | G7 | E7 • |
O ho-ly Child of Beth-le-hem,   Des-cend to/ us, we pray;

| • Am | G7 | F | C | E7 | C • |
Cast out our sin and en-ter in,   Be born in/ us to-day.

| Am | E7 | G7 • | F | Am | E7 • |
We hear the Christ-mas an-gels   The great glad tid-ings tell:

| C | Am | G7 | F | G7 | E7 | C ↓ |
Oh, come to us, a-bide with us,   Our Lord Em-man-u-el!

HH Singer, pg 50   CHRISTMAS   31

OF THE FATHER's LOVE BEGOTTEN

↓ ↑ _ ↑   Text: *Corde natus ex Parentis* by Aurelius C. Prudentius, 413; translated by John M. Neal, 1854
4 *r m i t*   Music: 87 87 87 7 DIVINUM MYSTERIUM, 12th C. chant, Mode V
3 A C E G
open C

SLOWLY

**① **

```
C        Am        C        Am  F↓   C         G7          C   ↓  G7↓
Of the Fa-ther's love be-got\-ten  Ere the worlds be-gan\ to be,
 F       Am        C        Am  F↓   Am        F           G7  ↓  C↓
He is Al-pha and O-me\-ga,    He the Source, the End\-ing he,
  •      Am        C        G7       C   ↓  G7↓
Of the things that are, that have / \ \ /  been,
 C       Am        C        G7↓  C        Am        C   G7  C↓
And that fu-ture years shall see  Ev-er-more and ev-er-more \.
```

**② **

```
 C       Am        C        Am  F↓   C         G7          C   ↓  G7↓
This the birth for-ev-er bless\-ed  When the Vir-gin, full\ of grace
 F       Am        C        Am  F↓   Am        F           G7  ↓  C↓
By the Ho-ly Ghost con-ceiv\-ing   Bore the Sa-vior of\ our race
  •      Am        C        G7       C   ↓  G7↓
And the Babe, the world's Re-deem / \ \ / -er,
 C       Am        C        G7↓  C        Am        C   G7  C↓
First re-vealed his sa-cred face  Ev-er-more and ev-er-more \.
```

**③ **

```
 C       Am        C        Am  F↓   C         G7          C   ↓  G7↓
He of whom the in-spired sing\-ers  Sang of old with one\ ac-cord,
 F       Am        C        Am  F↓   Am        F           G7  ↓  C↓
He whom voic-es of the proph\-ets Prom-ised in their faith\-ful word:
  •      Am        C        G7       C   ↓  G7↓
Now he shines, the long-ex-pec / \ \ / -ted.
 C       Am        C        G7↓  C        Am        C   G7  C↓
Let cre - a - tion praise its Lord  Ev-er-more and ev-er-more \.
```

32 CHRISTMAS HH Singer, pg 38

RISE UP SHEPHERD AND FOLLOW

²₂
↓↑ ↓↑
4 r m i t
3 A C E G
3ʳᵈ fret A

Text: African-American spiritual
Music: 10 7 11 7 with refrain

1

        C   •   G7   C
There's a star in the East on/ Christ-mas morn,
 G7   C7   F   C↓
Rise up, shep-herd, and fol-low.
     •   •   G7   C
It will lead to the place where the Christ was born\\,
  •   G7   F   C↓
Rise up, shep-herd, and fol-low.

REFRAIN
    • • G7 •
Fol/-low, fol\-low,
   •   C7   F   C↓
Rise up, shep-herd, and fol-low.
   •   G7   F Am
Fol-low the Star of Beth-le-hem\\,
  C   G7   F   C↓
Rise up, shep-herd, and fol-low.

2

     C   •   G7   C
If you take good\ heed to the an-gel's words,
 G7   C7   F   C↓
Rise up, shep-herd, and fol-low.
    •   •   G7   C
You'll for-get your\ flocks, you'll for-get your herds\\\,
  •   G7   F   C↓
Rise up, shep-herd, and fol-low.

REFRAIN

HH Singer, pg 29   CHRISTMAS   33

SILENT NIGHT

$^6_8$
↓ ↑ ↓
4 *t r i m*   or   *t m i r m i*
3   A E C A E G (*3 finger roll*)
2nd fret C
SLOW

Text: Joseph Mohr, 1818; translator unknown, altered
Music: STILLE NACHT, Franz Guber, 1818

**① **

G   •   •   •   D   •   G   •
Si/-lent night!   Ho/-ly night!   All is calm, all is bright,
   C   •   G   •
Round yon Vir\-gin Moth-er and Child.
   C   •   G   •
Ho-ly In-fant, so ten-der and mild,
  D   D7   G   •   •   D7   G   ↓
Sleep in heav-en-ly peace/,   Sleep\ in heav-en-ly peace.

**② **

G   •   •   •   D   •   G   •
Si/-lent night!   Ho/-ly night!   Shep-herds quake at the sight;
   C   •   G   •
Glo-ries stream\ from heav-en a-far,
   C   •   G   •
Heav'n-ly hosts\ sing, Al-le-lu-ia.
  D   D7   G   •   •   D7   G   ↓
Christ, the Sa-vior is born/!   Christ\, the Sa-vior is born!

**③ **

G   •   •   •   D   •   G   •
Si/-lent night!   Ho/-ly night!   Son of God, love's pure light
   C   •   G   •
Ra-diant beams\ form your ho-ly face,
   C   •   G   •
With the dawn of re-deem/-ing grace,
  D   D7   G   •   •   D7   G   ↓
Je-sus, Lord at your birth/,   Je\-sus, Lord at your birth.

34   CHRISTMAS   HH Singer, pg 55

THE FIRST NOEL

3/4

↓_↓↑↓_ ←
4 tr m i
3 A E C A E G
open E

Text: Traditional English Carol, 17th C., possibly 13th C.;
Music: Irregular

      C   G7   C   G7

① **The\ first/ No/-el, the/ an-gel did say,**

        C   G7   C   E7

Was to cer-tain poor shep-herds in fields as they lay;

      C   G7   C   G7

In\ fields/ where/ they lay/ keep-ing their sheep,

      C   G7   C   E7

On a cold win-ter's night/ that was\ so deep.

          C   G7   F   C

REFRAIN   **No\-el/, No/-el, No\-el, No-el,**

        F   C   F   C   ↓

Born is the King/ of Is\-ra-el.

     •   G7   C   G7

② **They\ look/-ed/ up and/ saw\ a star**

      C   G7   C   E7

Shin-ing in\ the east/, be-yond\ them far,

      C   G7   C   G7

And\ to/ the/ earth it/ gave\ great light,

      C   G7   C   E7

And/ so it con-tin-ued both day\ and night.

     •   G7   C   G7

③ **And\ by/ the/ light of/ that\ same star**

      C   G7   C   E7

Three/ ma\-gi came/ from coun\-try far;

      C   G7   C   G7

To\ seek/ for a king was/ their\ in-tent,

      C   G7   C   E7

And to fol-low the star/ wher-ev-er it went.   *REFRAIN*

```
              C         G7       F        C
REFRAIN    No\-el/, No/-el, No\-el, No-el,
             F          C        F     C     ↓
           Born is the King/ of Is\-ra-el.
```

```
            •         G7         C             G7
④  This\ star/ drew/ nigh un/-to the north-west,
         C        G7         C           E7
   O'er Beth\-le-hem/ it took\ its rest;
           C        G7            C         G7
   And\ there/ it/ did both/ stop\ and stay,
         C       G7         C           E7
   Right/ o-ver the place/ where Je\-sus lay.
```

```
            •        G7        C         G7
⑤  Then\ en/-tered/ in those/ ma\-gi three,
         C       G7          C        E7
   Full/ rev\-'rent-ly / up-on\ their knee,
          C         G7             C        G7
   And\ off/-ered/ there, in his pres\\-ence,
          C      G7          C          E7
   Their/ gold\ and myrrh/ and frank\-in-cense.          REFRAIN
```

```
            •         G7        C        G7
⑥  Then\ let/ us/ all with/ one\ ac-cord
         C       G7          C         E7
   Sing/ prais\-es to/ our heav\-'nly Lord;
         C       G7           C        G7
   Who\ with/ the/ Fa-ther/ we\ a-dore
         C       G7        C          E7
   And/ Spir\-it blest/ for ev\-er more.                 REFRAIN
```

36   CHRISTMAS   HH Singer, pg 42

THE GOD WHOM EARTH AND SEA AND SKY

C 4/4
↓ ↑ _ ↑
4 r m i t
3 A C E G
open A (low)

Text: Venantius Fortunatus, *Quem terra, pontus...*, d.609;
translated by John M. Neale, 1854, altered
Music option: ERHALT UNS HERR, LM; Klug's *Geistliche Lieder, 1543*;
Popular melody for: *The Glory Of These Forty Days*, page 56

(1)
```
      C            E7         C          F
The/ God whom\ earth and/ sea and sky
      G7      Am       G7       Am
A-dore and laud and mag-ni-fy,
         F        C        G7           C
Who o'er their/ three\-fold fab\-ric reigns,
       F       C        Dm       Am     •
The vir-gin's spot-less womb con-tains.
```

(2)
```
      C            E7         C          F
The/ God whose\ will by/ moon and sun
      G7      Am       G7       Am
And all things in due course is done,
         F        C        G7           C
Is borne up/-on\ a maid\-en's breast,
       F       C        Dm       Am     •
By full-est heav'-nly grace pos-sessed.
```

(3)
```
      C            E7         C          F
Blest/ in the\ mes-sage/ Ga-briel brought;
      G7      Am       G7       Am
Blest by the work the Spir-it wrought:
         F        C        G7           C
The Great De/-sire\ of all\ the earth
       F       C        Dm       Am     •
```

(4)
```
Took hu-man flesh and hu-man birth.

     C        E7       C     F      G7      Am      G7      Am
All/ ho-nor\, laud, and/ glo-ry be,  To you, O Je-sus, of the Three,
     F       C      G7     C        F       C       Dm      Am
All glo-ry/, as\ you ev\-er meet  Our Fa-ther and the Pa-ra-clete.
```

VIRGIN-BORN WE BOW BEFORE YOU

Text: Reginald Heber, d.1826, altered for a different tune
Music: 88 7 STABAT MATER, *Mainz Gesanbuch,* 1661

C 4/4
↓ _ ↓ ↑
4 r m i t
3 A C E G
open C

1.
    C   Am •   F   C↓
Vir-gin-**born**, we bow be-fore you;
   • Am   F   Am   G7↓
Bless-ed was the womb that bore you:
   • E7   G7   C↓
Ma-ry, Moth-er meek and mild.

2.
  • Am •   F   C↓
Bless-ed was the maid that fed you;
  • Am   F   Am   G7↓
Bless-ed was the hand that led you;
  • E7   G7   C↓
Watch-ing you, the in-fant child.

3.
  • Am •   F   C↓
Bless-ed she by all cre-a-tion,
  • Am   F   Am   G7↓
Who brought forth the world's sal-va-tion;
  • E7   G7   C↓
Bless-ed was her par-ent style.

4.
  • Am •   F   C↓
Bless-ed was she in her Chi-ld.
  • Am   F   Am   G7↓
Bless-ed they for-ev-er blest, who
  • E7   G7   C↓
Love you most and serve you while.

5. *Repeat First Verse.*

38   CHRISTMAS   HH Singer, pg 119

SONGS OF THANKFULNESS AND PRAISE

C $^4_8$

↓ _ ↓ ↑
4   *r m i t*
3   A G E C

open G

Text: Christopher Wordsworth, 1862, altered
Music: 77 77 D, SALZBURG; Jakob Hintze, 1678; adapted by Johann Sebastian Bach, d. 1750

(1)

```
         C              G7          •              C
       Songs  of thank-ful-ness  and  praise,
         G7            F         Dm          C
       Je-sus,  Lord,  to  you  we  raise,
  •     G7      •        C       G7       F        Dm       C
Man-i-fest-ed  by  the  star    To  the  ma-gi  from  a-far;
 G7     G6      C        G7      F         C       E7       Am
Branch of roy/-al Da-vid's stem  In  your  birth  at  Beth-le-hem;
  C      F       C        G7     Am        F       G7       C
Prais-es be to you ad-dressed,   God in flesh made man-i-fest.
```

(2)

```
  •     G7      •                C
     Man-i-fest at Jor-dan's stream,
         G7            F         Dm          C
       Pro-phet, Priest and King su-preme;
  •     G7      •        C       G7       F        Dm       C
And as Ca-na's wed-ding guest,  In your God-head man-i-fest;
 G7     G6      C        G7      F         C       E7       Am
Man-i-fest/ in pow'r div-ine,   Chang-ing wa-ter in-to wine;
  C      F       C        G7     Am        F       G7       C
Prais-es be to you ad-dressed,   God in flesh made man-i-fest.
```

(3)

```
  •     G7      •        C       G7       F        Dm       C
Grant us grace to see you, Lord, Mir-rored in your ho-ly Word;
  •     G7   •           C       G7       F        Dm       C
May our im-i-ta-tion show,     In your like-ness may we go;
 G7     G6      C        G7     F          C       E7       Am
Pure and ho/-ly may we be      At your great E-pi-pha-ny;
  C      F       C        G7     Am        F       G7       C
May we praise you, ev-er blest,  God in flesh made man-i-fest.
```

CHRISTMAS   39

WE THREE KINGS OF ORIENT ARE

HH Singer, pg 54

$^3_8$
↓_ ↓ ↑ ↓_
4 tr m i
3 A E C A E G
open E

Text: from Matthew 2:1-11, John H. Hopkins, Jr., 1857, altered
Music: 88 44 6 KINGS OF ORIENT with refrain, John H. Hopkins, Jr., 1857

❶

| Am | • | E7 | Am | • | • | E7 | Am |

We three kings of O-ri-ent are; Bear-ing gifts we tra-verse a-far,

| C | G7 | Am | F | Dm | E7 | Am • |

Field and foun-tain, moor and moun\-tain, Fol-low-ing yon-der star.

REFRAIN

| G7 • | C | • | F | C | • | • | F | C |

O / star of won-der, star of night, Star with roy-al beau-ty bright,

| • | G7 | F | G7 |

West-ward lead-ing, still pro-ceed-ing,

| C | • | F | C | Am↓ |

Guide us to your per-fect Light.

❷

| • | • | E7 | Am | • | • | E7 | Am |

Born a King on Beth-le-hem's plain Gold I bring to crown him a-gain,

| C | G7 | Am | F | Dm | E7 | Am | • |

King for-ev-er, ceas-ing nev\-er, O-ver us all to reign.   *REFRAIN*

❸

| • | • | E7 | Am | • | • | E7 | Am |

Frank-in-cense to of-fer have I; In-cense owns a De-i-ty nigh;

| C | G7 | Am | F | Dm | E7 | Am • |

Prayer and prais-ing, voic-es rais\-ing, Wor-ship-ping God on high.

REFRAIN

❹

| • | • | E7 | Am | • | • | E7 | Am |

Myrrh is mine, its bit-ter per-fume Breathes a life of gath-er-ing gloom;

| C | G7 | Am | F | Dm | E7 | Am • |

Sorr'w-ing, sigh-ing, bleed-ing, dy\-ing, Sealed in the stone cold tomb.

REFRAIN

❺

| • | • | E7 | Am | • | • | E7 | Am |

Glo-rious now be-hold him a-rise; King and God and sac/-ri-fice;

| C | G7 | Am | F | Dm | E7 | Am • |

Al-le-lu-ia! Al-le-lu\-ia! Sounds through the earth and skies. *REFRAIN*

40   CHRISTMAS   HH Singer, pg 47

WHAT CHILD IS THIS

$^6_4$

↓ ↑ ↓

4 *tr m i* 3 AG E C

open A (low)

Text: William C. Dix, *The Manger Throne*, 1865
Music: 87 87 GREENSLEEVES with refrain, English Melody, 16th C.

**① **

SLOW Am • G7 • F • E7 •
What child is this/ who, laid to rest/ On Ma-ry's lap\ is sleep\-ing?
    Am • G7 •
Whom an-gels greet/ with an-thems sweet/,
    Am E7 Am •
While shep\-herds watch\ are keep-ing?
  C • G7 • Am • E7 •
This, this\ is Christ the King/, Whom shep-herds guard\ and an-gels sing;
  C • G7 • Am E7 Am •
Haste, haste\, to bring him laud/, The Babe\, the Son\ of Ma-ry.

**② **

  Am • G7 • F • E7 •
Why lies he in/ such mean e-state/, Where ox and ass\ are feed\-ing?
    Am • G7 •
Good Christ-ians, fear/, for sin-ners here/
  Am E7 Am •
The si\-lent Word\ is plead-ing.
  C • G7 • Am • E7 •
Nails, spear\ shall pierce him through/, The cross be borne\ for me, for you.
  C • G7 • Am E7 Am •
Hail, hail\ the Word made flesh/, The Babe\, the Son\ of Ma-ry.

**③ **

  Am • G7 • F • E7 •
So bring him in/-cense, gold and myrrh/, Come peas-ant, king\ to greet\ him;
  Am • G7 •
The King of kings/ sal-va-tion brings/,
  Am E7 Am •
Let lov\-ing hearts\ en-throne him.
  C • G7 • Am • E7 •
Raise, raise\ a song on high/, The vir-gin sings\ her lul-la-by.
  C • G7 • Am E7 Am •
Joy, joy\ for Christ is born/, The Babe\, the Son\ of Ma-ry.

HH Singer, pg 58 — CHRISTMAS — 41

LO, HOW A ROSE E'ER BLOOMING

Text: based on Isaiah 11:1; traditional German carol, 15th century;
translated by Theodore Baker, 1851-1934, altered
Music: 76 76 6 76 ES IST EIN' ROS' ENTSPRUNGEN,
Alte Catholische Geistliche Kirchengesange, Cologne, 1599

↓ ↑ _ ↑
4 *r m i t*
3 A C E G
open G
SLOWLY

1

```
  C    G6        F          C  Am    F  Am↓↑ G7 Am G7↓↑   C      ↓
Lo, how a Rose e'er bloom-ing From ten-der stem hath sprung!
  •    G6        F          C  Am    F  Am↓↑ G7 Am G7↓↑   C      ↓
Of Jes-se's lin-eage com-ing,  As those of old have sung.
         G7        C      G7       ↓
It came, a flow-er bright,
         C         F      C  Am    F  Am↓↑ G7 Am G7↓↑   C      ↓
A-mid the cold of win-ter,   When half spent was the night.
```

2

```
  C    G6        F          C  Am    F  Am↓↑ G7 Am G7↓↑   C      ↓
I - sai-ah 'twas fore-told it,  This Rose I have in  mind,
  •    G6        F          C  Am    F  Am↓↑ G7 Am G7↓↑   C      ↓
With Ma-ry we be-hold it,    The Vir-gin Moth-er kind.
         G7        C      G7       ↓
To show God's love a-right,
         C         F      C  Am    F  Am↓↑ G7 Am G7↓↑   C      ↓
She bore to us a Sav-ior,    When half-spent was the night.
```

3

```
  C    G6        F          C  Am    F  Am↓↑ G7 Am G7↓↑ C ↓
O Flow'r, whose fra-grance ten-der With sweet-ness fills the air,
  •    G6        F          C  Am    F  Am↓↑ G7 Am G7↓↑   C      ↓
Dis-pel in glo-rious splen-dor   The dark-ness ev-'ry-where;
         G7        C      G7       ↓
True man, yet ver-y God,
         C         F      C  Am    F  Am↓↑ G7 Am G7↓↑   C      ↓
From sin and death now save us, And share our ev-'ry load.
```

42   LENT   HH Singer, pg 110

ALL GLORY LAUD AND HONOR

C 4/4
↓ ↑ _ ↑
4 tr m i m
3 A C E G
open G (low)

Text: St. Theodulph of Orleans, 821?, for Palm Sunday;
translated by John M. Neal, 1854, altered
Music: 76 76 D, ST. THEODULPH, Melchior Teschner, 1613

1

```
     C     G7    F  •      C       F    •  Am
All glo-ry, laud, and hon-or,  to you, re-deem-er, King,
     C     G7    F  •      C    Am      F  Am
To whom the lips of chil-dren  make sweet ho-san-nas ring.
     F     C     E7   Am      F     G7    C    C7
The King you are of Is-ra-el,  and Da-vid's roy-al Son,
   Am    G7    C   Am       C7    G7      F   ↓
Be-lov-ed of the Fa\-ther,  our Roy-al Bless-ed One.
```

2

```
     C     G7    F  •      C       F    •  Am
The com-pa-ny of an-gels   are prais-ing you on high,
     C     G7    F  •      C     Am     F  Am
With hu-man be-ings too all  cre-a-tion makes re-ply.
     F     C     E7   Am      F     G7      C  C7
The Cho-sen of the Cov-e-nant  with psalms be-fore you went;
   Am    G7    C    Am      C7    G7      F   ↓
So too our praise and an\-thems  be-fore you we pre-sent.
```

3

```
     C     G7    F  •      C       F    •   Am
To you, be-fore your pass-ion,  a-pos-tles sang your praise;
     C     G7    F  •      C    F       •  Am
To you, now high ex-al-ted,  our mel-o-dy we raise.
     F     C     E7   Am        F     G7      C   C7
Ac-cep-ta-ble their voi\-ces;  hear too the praise we bring:
   Am    G7    C    Am      C7    G7      F   ↓
De-light in your be-lov\-ed,  our Sa-vior and our King.
```

AT THE NAME OF JESUS

Text: See Philippians 3:6-11; Caroline M. Noel, *The Name of Jesus and Other Verses for the Sick and Lonely*, 1870, altered
Music: 11 11 11 11 ADORO TE DEVOTE, Benedictine Plainsong, Mode V, 13th Century

C 3/4
↓ ↑ ↓
4 tr m i 3 AG E C
Claw A ↓ G
open C

1.
| C | G7 | • | • | F | G7 | C | ↓ |
At the name of Je/-sus, ev-'ry knee shall bow,
| C | G7 | • | • | F | G7 | C | ↓ |
Ev-'ry tongue con-fess/ him King of glo-ry now;
| G7 | F | C | G7 | F | Dm | E7 | ↓ |
'Tis the Fa/-ther's plea\-sure that we call him Lord,
| C | F | Dm | • | C | G7 | C | ↓ |
Who from the be-gin\-ning is the migh-ty Word.

2.
| C | G7 | • | • | F | G7 | C | ↓ |
At his voice cre-a/-tion sprang at once to sight,
| C | G7 | • | • | F | G7 | C | ↓ |
All the an-gels' fa/-ces, all the hosts of light,
| G7 | F | C | G7 | F | Dm | E7 | ↓ |
Thrones and dom/-in-a\-tions, stars up-on their way,
| C | F | Dm | • | C | G7 | C | ↓ |
All the heav'n-ly or\-ders, in their great ar-ray.

3.
| C | G7 | • | • | F | G7 | C | ↓ |
Hum-bled for a sea/-son, to re-ceive a name
| C | G7 | • | • | F | G7 | C | ↓ |
From the lips of sin/-ners un-to whom he came,
| G7 | F | C | G7 | F | Dm | E7 | ↓ |
Faith-ful-ly/ he bore\ it, spot-less to the last,
| C | F | Dm | • | C | G7 | C | ↓ |
Carr-ied it vic-tor\-ious when from death he passed.

4.
| C | G7 | • | • | F | G7 | C | ↓ |
Bro-thers, Sis-ters, name/ him, with love strong as death
| C | G7 | • | • | F | G7 | C | ↓ |
But with awe and won/-der, and with halt-ed breath!
| G7 | F | C | G7 | F | Dm | E7 | ↓ |
He is God/ our Sa\-vior, he is Christ the Lord,
| C | F | Dm | • | C | G7 | C | ↓ |
Ev-er to be wor\-shipped, trust-ed and a-dored.

44   LENT   HH Singer, pgs 74,75

O MY GOD MY GOD WHY

Text: Psalm 22, by Stephen J. Wolf, 2006, tribute to the priesthood of William J. Fleming
Music: 11 11 11 11 ADORO TE DEVOTE, Benedictine Plainsong, Mode V, 13th Century

C 3/4
↓ ↑ ↓
4 tr m i
3 AG E C
Claw A ↓ G
open C

1
```
C       G7    •       •     F    G7       C    ↓
O my God, my God, why have you a-ban-doned me?
C       G7    •       •     F    G7       C    ↓
Why so far from cries for help, rest-less an-guish call?
G7      F     C       G7    F    Dm       E7   ↓
God, my God/, I call by day, no re-ply to hear.
C       F     Dm      •     C    G7       C    ↓
God, my God, I call by night, no re-lief, I fear.
```

2
```
C       G7    •       •     F    G7       C    ↓
Yet en-throned, our Ho-ly One God of Is-ra-el,
C       G7    •       •     F    G7       C    ↓
Trust-ed by an-ces-tors you gave a place to dwell.
G7      F     C       G7    F    Dm       E7   ↓
They cried out/ to you in need, beg-ging to be free,
C       F     Dm      •     C    G7       C    ↓
Call-ing on their source of hope, free you let them be.
```

3
```
C       G7    •       •     F    G7       C    ↓
They say I am like a worm, hard-ly hu-man, scorned,
C       G7    •       •     F    G7       C    ↓
Mocked, de-spised by ev-'ry-one, tar-get of their fun.
G7      F     C       G7    F    Dm       E7   ↓
All who see/ me mock and scorn, curl their lips and jeer:
C       F     Dm      •     C    G7       C    ↓
"Let your Lord de-liv-er you, save you from your fear."
```

4
```
C       G7    •       •     F    G7       C    ↓
From the womb you drew me forth, safe-ty at the breast;
C       G7    •       •     F    G7       C    ↓
From the womb on you I fell, from my birth your guest.
G7      F     C       G7    F    Dm       E7   ↓
Stay not far/ a-way from me, God, my God since birth;
C       F     Dm      •     C    G7       C    ↓
Near are fear and troub-le now, help-less I go forth.
```

5
```
C       G7    •       •     F    G7       C    ↓
Wi-ld bulls sur-round a-round, brag-ging on their horns.
C       G7    •       •     F    G7       C    ↓
Li-ons fierce en-cir-cle me, rend a-bout and roar.
G7      F     C       G7    F    Dm       E7   ↓
Drain-ing life/ like wa-ter soft, I can bare-ly speak.
C       F     Dm      •     C    G7       C    ↓
Melt-ed is my heart, like wax, all my bones grow weak.
```

LENT

⑥
```
    C        G7    •    •      F        G7      C    ↓
Dry as bro-ken bits of pots  are my mouth and throat;
    C        G7    •    •      F        G7      C    ↓
Dry tongue stuck in-side my mouth,  tast-ing dust and dirt.
  G7       F        C     G7     F       Dm      E7   ↓
I can count/ up bone by bone,  wa-sted hands and feet;
    C      F       Dm    •     C       G7      C    ↓
Pack of dogs close in on me,  dogs a-foot com-pete.
```

⑦
```
    C        G7    •    •      F        G7      C    ↓
At my life they stare and gloat,  at my life torn up,
    C        G7    •    •      F        G7      C    ↓
For my clo-thing cast-ing lots,  gar-ments rip-ping up.
  G7       F        C     G7     F       Dm      E7   ↓
Save me from/ the li-on mouth,  dogs and bulls and sword.
    C      F       Dm    •     C       G7      C    ↓
Quick-ly, help, de-liv-er me  from this gath-ered hoard.
```

⑧
```
    C        G7    •    •      F        G7      C    ↓
Then will I pro-claim your name  in com-mu-nit-y!
    C        G7    •    •      F        G7      C    ↓
In as-semb-ly, praise your name,  this vow I will keep;
  G7       F        C     G7     F       Dm      E7   ↓
"Ja-cob now/ named Is-ra-el, all de-scend-ants call:
    C      F       Dm    •     C       G7      C    ↓
All who fear the Lord, give praise!  Hal-le-lu-jah all!
```

⑨
```
    C        G7    •    •      F        G7      C    ↓
"God did not spurn this one poor  soul of mis-er-y,
    C        G7    •    •      F        G7      C    ↓
Did not hide the face from mine,  heard my cry in need.
  G7       F        C     G7     F       Dm      E7   ↓
All God's poor/ will eat their fill,  all the an-a-wim,
    C      F       Dm    •     C       G7      C    ↓
Off-er praise and seek the Lord,  hearts a-live in him."
```

⑩
```
    C        G7    •    •      F        G7      C    ↓
From the edg-es of the earth  all will wor-ship God,
    C        G7    •    •      F        G7      C    ↓
Fam-il-ies and na-tions all  turn-ing to the Lord.
  G7       F        C     G7     F       Dm      E7   ↓
All king-ship/ be-longs to God,  ru-ler of us all.
    C      F       Dm    •     C       G7      C    ↓
All the liv-ing and the dead  low in hom-age fall.
```

⑪
```
    C        G7    •    •      F        G7      C    ↓
All who sleep in earth and dust  bow in hom-age, kneel.
    C        G7    •    •      F        G7      C    ↓
All de-scend-ants, serve the Lord,  live for God, live well.
  G7       F        C     G7     F       Dm      E7   ↓
Tell each gen/-er-a-tion next  of the Lord you've known,
    C      F       Dm    •     C       G7      C    ↓
Teach de-liv-er-ance to all  peo-ple to be born.
```

46 CROWN HIM WITH MANY CROWNS

LENT HH Singer, pg 71

C 4/4
↓ _ ↓ ↑
4 r m i t
3 A G E C
open C
SLOWLY

Text: From Revelation 19:12; verses for Lent by Matthew Bridges, 1851, altered
Music: DIADEMATA, George J. Elvey, 1868

(for Lent)

1

```
    C              Am       F  •    C         F        G7    •
Crown him with ma-ny crowns   The Lamb up-on his throne;
    C         F        D         G7        Am       F      G7 •
Hark how the heav'n-ly an-them\ drowns All mu-sic but its own.
    C             G7      F  Am     F        G7      E7     G7
A-wake, my soul, and sing    Of him who died for thee
    C        F        G7      C              F      G7      C   •
And hail him as your King of kings  Through all e-ter-ni-ty.
```

2

```
     •           Am       F  •    C         F        G7    •
Crown him the Lord of Love.  Be-hold his hands and side,
    C          F       D       G7       Am       F       G7  •
Rich wounds, yet vis-ib-le a\-bove,  In beau-ty glo-ri-fied.
    C            G7      F  Am     F        G7      E7     G7
No an-gel in the sky    Can ful-ly bear that sight,
    C          F          G7        C          F       G7       C •
But down-ward bends his wond'-ring eye  At mys-te-ry so bright!
```

3

```
     •           Am        F  •    C         F        G7    •
Crown him the Lord of Life   Who tri-umphed o'er the grave
    C            F       D        G7       Am         F       G7 •
And rose vic-to-rious in the\ strife  For those he came to save.
    C           G7      F  Am     F       G7       E7     G7
His glo-ries now we sing    Who died and rose on high,
    C         F          G7       C         F       G7         C  •
Who died e-ter-nal life to bring  And lives that death may die.
```

47

HH Singer, pg 64 — LENT

FORTY DAYS AND FORTY NIGHTS

Text: George H. Smyttan, *The Penny Post*, 1856, altered
Music: 7 7 7 7 HEINLEIN, Attributed to Martin Herbst, d. 1681

C 4/4
↓ _ ↓ ↑
4 r m i t
3 A C E G

open E

1

```
      C        F        Am       C
For-ty days and for-ty nights
   •          G7       F        E7
You were fast-ing in the wild;
   •          F        G7       C
For-ty days and for-ty nights
   •          G7       E7       Am    ↓
Temp-ted, and yet un-de-filed.
```

2

```
      C        F        Am       C
Should not we your sor-row share
   •          G7       F        E7
And from world-ly joys ab-stain,
   •          F        G7       C
Fast-ing with un-ceas-ing prayer,
   •          G7       E7       Am    ↓
Strong with you to suf-fer pain?
```

3

```
    C    F    Am    C      •   G7    F      E7
When temp-ta-tions on us press,  Je-sus, Sa-vior, hear our call!
  •   F    G7    C    •   G7    E7    Am    ↓
Vic-tor in the wil-der-ness, Grant we may not faint nor fall!
```

4

```
    C    F    Am    C      •   G7    F      E7
Keep, O keep us, Sa-vior dear,  Ev-er con-stant by your side;
  •   F    G7    C    •   G7    E7    Am    ↓
That with you we may ap-pear  At th'e-ter-nal Eas-ter-tide.
```

48   LENT   HH Singer, pg 59

LORD WHO THROUGHOUT THESE FORTY DAYS

C 4/4
↓ ↑ _ ↑
4 r m i t
3 A C E G
open C

Text: Claudia F. Hernaman, *Child's Book of Praise: A Manuel of Devotion*, 1873, altered
Music: ST. FLAVIAN, CM, *Day's Psalter*, 1563

1

    C   F   G7   C   F   G7   E7 Am
Lord, who through-out these for-ty days For us did fast and pray,
 •   G7   C   E7   G7   F   C ↓
Teach us with you to mourn our sins And close by you to stay.

2

 •   F   G7   C   F   G7   E7 Am
As you with Sa-tan did con-tend, And did the vic-t'ry win,
 •   G7   C   E7   G7   F   C ↓
O give us strength in you to fight, In you to con-quer sin.

3

 •   F   G7   C   F   G7   E7 Am
As you did hun-ger bear, and thirst, So teach us, gra-cious Lord,
 •   G7   C   E7   G7   F   C ↓
To die to self, and so to live In your most ho-ly Word.

4

       •   F   G7   C
And through these days of pen-i-tence,
      F   G7   E7   Am
And in your Pas-chal Way,
    •   G7   C   E7
Yes, ev-er-more through life and death,
    G7   F   C ↓
Lord Je-sus, with us stay

5

 •   F   G7   C   F   G7   E7 Am
A-bide with us, and when this life With suf-fer-ing has passed
 •   G7   C   E7   G7   F   C ↓
An East-er of un-end-ing joy May we at-tain at last.

HH Singer, pg 138 — LENT — 49

O SAVING VICTIM

3/4
↓↑↓ or ↓_↓
4 tr m i
3 AG E C
open G (low)

Text: Thomas Aquinas, 1227-74; O SALUTARIS HOSTIA,
translated by Edward Caswall, 1849, altered
Music: WERNER (O SALUTARIS HOSTIA), Anthony Werner, 1863
see *Peoples Mass Book* #677, WLP, 1984

1

```
     C           F      Dm        C
O sav-ing Vic-tim, o-pen wide
  •              G7      F        C
The gate of heav'n to us\ be-low;
  •                    Am      F       G7
Our foes press on / from ev-'ry side;
  C             Am            E7         C
Your aid sup-ply\; your strength be-stow.
```

2

```
  •              F      Dm        C
To your great Name be end-less praise;
  •              G7      F        C
Im-mort-al God-head, One\ in Three;
  •              Am      F       G7
Grant us for end/-less length of days,
  C             Am           E7         C
In our true na\-tive land to be.
```

3

```
  •              F      Dm        C
O sa-lu-ta-ris Ho-sti-a,
  •              G7      F        C
Quae cae-li pan-dis o\-sti-um:
  •              Am      F       G7
Bel-la pre-munt/ ho-sti-li-a,
  C             Am           E7         C        •  •
Da ro-bur fer\ au-xi-li-um.              A-men.
```

50 — O SACRED HEAD NOW WOUNDED

LENT · HH Singer, pg 69

C 4/4
↓ ↑ _ ↑
4 *m r t i t*
3 A C E G
open E

Text: possibly Bernard of Clairvaux, 1153; translated to English by James W. Alexander, 1830, altered
Music: 76 76 D PASSION CHORALE, Hans L. Hassler, 1601

Try Capo on the 2nd fret

1

| F | Dm | G7 | C |
O Sa-cred Head, now wound-ed
 • E7   F ↓
With grief and shame\ weighed down,
 • Dm G7 C • E7 F ↓
Now scorn-ful-ly sur-round-ed With thorns, your on\-ly crown.
 G7 F C • F Dm E7 ↓
They mock\ and taunt and jeer you, Your no-ble coun-ten-ance,
 G7 C Am E7 Dm G7 C ↓
Though migh/-ty worlds shall fear you And flee be-fore your glance.

2

 F Dm G7 C • E7 F ↓
My bur-den in your pas-sion, Lord, you have borne\ for me.
 • Dm G7 C • E7 F ↓
For it was my trans-gres-sion Which brought this woe\ on thee.
 G7 F C • F Dm E7 ↓
I cast\ me down be-fore you, Wrath were my right-ful lot;
 G7 C Am E7 Dm G7 C ↓
Have mer/-cy, I im-plore you; Re-deem-er, spurn me not!

3

 F Dm G7 C • E7 F ↓
What lang-uage shall I bor-row To thank you, dear\-est friend,
 • Dm G7 C • E7 F ↓
For this your dy-ing sor-row, Your pit-y with\-out end?
 G7 F C • F Dm E7 ↓
O make\ me yours for-ev-er, And should I faint-ing be,
 G7 C Am E7 Dm G7 C ↓
Lord, let/ me nev-er, nev-er Out-live my love to thee.

HH Singer, pg 124   LENT   51

O SACRED HEAD SURROUNDED

C 4/4
↓ ↑ _ ↑
4 *mr t i t*
3 A C E G
open E

Text: Ascribed to Bernard of Clairvaux, 1091-1153; translated by Henry Baker, 1821-77
Music: 76 76 D PASSION CHORALE, Hans L. Hassler, 1601

Try Capo on the 2nd fret

①

   F   Dm   G7 C •   E7   F ↓
O Sa-cred Head, sur-round-ed   By crown of pierc\-ing thorn.
  •   Dm   G7 C •   E7   F ↓
O Bleed-ing Head, so wound-ed,   Re-viled and put\ to scorn.
  G7   F   C •   F   Dm   E7 ↓
If sins\ could mar the glo-ry Of your most ho-ly Face,
  G7   C   Am E7   Dm   G7   C ↓
Yet an/-gel hosts a-dor-ing,   They trem-ble as they gaze.

②

   F   Dm   G7 C •   E7   F ↓
I see your strength and vig-or   All fa-ding in\ the strife,
  •   Dm   G7 C •   E7   F ↓
And death with cru-el rig-or,   Be-reav-ing you\ of life;
  G7   F   C •   F   Dm   E7 ↓
O ag\-o-ny and dy-ing! O love to sin-ner's free!
  G7   C   Am E7   Dm   G7   C ↓
Je-sus/, all grace sup-ply-ing,   O turn your face on me.

③

   F   Dm   G7 C •   E7   F ↓
In this, your bit-ter pass-ion, Good Shep-herd, think\ of me
  •   Dm   G7 C •   E7   F ↓
With your most sweet com-pass-ion, un-wor-thy though\ I be:
  G7   F   C •   F   Dm   E7 ↓
Be-neath\ your cross a-bi-ding   For ev-er would I rest,
  G7   C   Am E7   Dm   G7   C ↓
In your/ dear love con-fi-ding,   And in your pres-ence blest.

52 — PRAISE TO THE HOLIEST IN THE HEIGHT

LENT — HH Singer, pg 60

C 4/4
↓ ↑ _ ↑ (lightly)
4 tr m i m
3 A C E G
open C

Text: from Psalm 148:1, John Henry Newman, *The Dream of Gerontius*, 1865, altered
Music: KINGSFOLD, CMD, traditional English melody, adapted by Ralph Vaughan Williams, 1906
Popular melody for: *I Heard the Voice of Jesus Say*, page 100

1

```
         F       Am       C        G7
Praise\ to the Ho-liest in the height,
         C        Dm            G7      •
And/ from the depth\ come praise;
         F       Am       C        G7
The\ words of God most won-der-ful,
         C        Dm           Am       •
Most/ sure are all\ God's ways.
         G7       C        F        Am
O/ lov-ing wis\-dom of our God!
         C        F        G7       •
When/ all was\ sin and shame,
         F       Am       C        G7
A\ sec-ond A-dam to the fight
         C        Dm       Am      ↓
And/ to the res\-cue came.
```

2

```
         F     Am      C      G7        C       Dm        G7   •
And\ in the gar-den se-cret-ly,   And/ from the Cross\ on high,
         F     Am      C      G7        C       Dm       Am    •
Should\ teach dis-cip-les, and in-spire  To/ suf-fer and\ to die.
         G7      C       F        Am
And/ that a high\-er gift than grace
         C       F       G7      •
Should/ flesh and\ blood re-fine,
         F       Am        C       G7       C       Dm      Am  ↓
God's\ Pres-ence and God's ve-ry Self, And/ Es-sence all di-vine.
```

HH Singer, pg 73 — LENT — 53

SING MY TONGUE THE SAVIOR's GLORY

C 4/4
↓ _ ↓ ↑
4 r m i t
3 A C E G
open C
SLOWLY

Text: Thomas Aquinas, *Pange lingua gloriosi*, d. 1274,
translated by Edward Caswell, 1849, altered
Music: 87 87 87 ST. THOMAS (TANTUM ERGO), John F. Wade, d.1786
Popular melody for: *Down In Adoration Falling*

    C   Am   F   Dm   C
Sing, my tongue, the Sa-vior's glo-ry,
  Am   Dm   G7   C
Of his flesh the mys-t'ry sing,
  •   •   F   Dm   C
Of the blood, all price ex-ceed-ing,
  Am   C   Am   G7
Shed by our im-mort-al King,
  •   C   G7   Dm   C
Des-tined, for the world's re-demp-tion,
  F   Dm   G7   C ↓
From a no-ble womb to spring.

C   Am   F   Dm   C Am Dm   G7   C
On the night of that Last Sup-per, Seat-ed with his cho-sen band,
  •   •   F   Dm   C Am C   Am   G7
He, the pas-chal vic-tim eat-ing, First ful-fills the law's com-mand;
  •   C   G7   Dm   C F   Dm   G7   C ↓
Then as food to all his sib-lings Gives him-self with his own hand.

3

C   Am   F   Dm   C Am Dm   G7   C
To the ev-er-last-ing Fa-ther, And the Son who made us free,
  •   •   F   Dm   C Am C   Am   G7
And the Spir-it, God pro-ceed-ing, From them each e-ter-nal-ly,
  •   C   G7   Dm   C F   Dm   G7   C ↓
Be sal-va-tion, hon-or, bless-ing, Might and end-less maj-es-ty.

54   LENT   HH Singer, pg 68

SOMEBODY'S KNOCKIN'

Text & Music: Traditional spiritual

$\frac{2}{4}$
↓ ↑ ↓ ↑
4 t i m r
3 A C E G
open C

   C   **F**   **C**   ·
Some-bo-dy's knock-in' at your door,
   G7   **F**   **G7**   ·
Some-bo-dy's knock-in' at your door,
 ·   **F**   **Am**   **C**
O/ sin-ner, why don't you an-swer?
 ·   **F**   **C**   ·
Some-bo-dy's knock-in' at your door.

 ·   ·   ·   **F**   **C** ·

(1) Knocks like Je-sus,   **Some-bo-dy's** knock-in' at your door,
     G7   ·
Knocks like\ Je-sus,

          G7   **F**   **G7**   ·
REFRAIN   Some-bo-dy's knock-in' at your door,
         ·   **F**   **Am**   **C**
         O/ sin-ner, why don't you an-swer?
         ·   **F**   **C** ·
         Some-bo-dy's knock-in' at your door,

 ·   ·   ·   **F**   **C** ·

(2) Can't you hear him? **Some-bo-dy's** knock-in' at your door,
     G7   ·
Can't you\ hear him?   **REFRAIN**

 ·   ·   ·   **F**   **C** ·

(3) An-swer Je-sus, **Some-bo-dy's** knock-in' at your door,
     G7   ·
An-swer\ Je-sus,   **REFRAIN**

WHEN I SURVEY THE WONDROUS CROSS

Text: Isaac Watts, Hymns and Spiritual Songs, 1707, altered
Music: HAMBURG, Lowel Mason, 1824;
The Boston Handel and Haydn Society Collection of Church Music, 1825

²₂
↓ ↑ _ ↑
4 r m i t r m i t
3 A C E G A C E G
open C

SLOWLY

**① **

```
  C           E7      F          C
When I sur-vey the/ won-drous\ cross
  •           G7      F          G7
On which the Prince of\ glo-ry/ died,
  C           E7      F          C
My rich-est gain I/ count as\ loss,
  •                   F     G7   C
And pour con-tempt on all my\ pride.
```

**② **

```
  C           E7      F          C
For-bid it, Lord, that/ I should\ boast,
  •           G7      F          G7
Save in the death of\ Christ my/ God!
  C           E7      F          C
May all vain things that/ charm me\ most,
  •                   F     G7   C
Be sac-ri-ficed as with his\ blood.
```

**③ **

```
  C           E7      F          C
Were the whole realm of/ na-ture\ mine,
  •           G7      F          G7
That trea-sure would be\ far too/ small;
  C           E7      F          C
Love so a-ma-zing/, so div\-ine,
  •                   F     G7   C
De-mands my soul, my life, my\ all.
```

56   LENT   HH Singer, pg 66

THE GLORY OF THESE FORTY DAYS

C 4/4

↓ ↑ _ ↑
4 r m i t
3 A C E G

open A (low)

Text: Gregory the Great, 6th Century,
translated by Maurice F. Bell, *The English Hymnal*, 1906, altered
Music option: ERHALT UNS HERR, LM; Klug's *Geistliche Lieder*, 1543

1

    C   E7   C   F
The/ glo-ry\ of these/ for-ty days
    G7   Am   G7   Am
We cel-e-brate with songs of praise;
    F   C   G7   C
For Christ, by/ whom\ all things\ were made,
    F   C   Dm   Am •
Him-self has fast-ed and has prayed.

2

    C   E7   C   F   G7   Am   G7   Am
A/-**lone** and\ fast-ing/ Mo-ses saw   The lov-ing God who gave the law;
    F   C   G7   C   F   C   Dm   Am •
And to E /-li \-jah, fast\-ing, came   The steeds and char-i-ots of flame.

3

    C   E7   C   F
So/ Dan-iel\ trained his/ mys-tic sight,
    G7   Am   G7   Am
De-liv-ered from the li-on's might;
    F   C   G7   C
And John, the/ Bride\-groom's friend\, be-came
    F   C   Dm   Am •
The her-ald of Mes-si-ah's Name.

4

    C   E7   C   F
Then/ grant us\, Lord, like/ them to be
    G7   Am   G7   Am
In faith-ful fast and prayer with thee;
    F   C   G7   C
Our spir-its/ strength\-en with\ your grace,
    F   C   Dm   Am •
And give us joy to see your face.

TAKE UP YOUR CROSS

Text: Charles W. Everest, *Visions of Death and Other Poems,* 1833, altered
Music option: ERHALT UNS HERR, LM; Klug's *Geistliche Lieder,* 1543
Popular melody for: *The Glory Of These Forty Days,* page 56

C 4/4
↓ ↑ _ ↑
4 *r m i t*
3 A C E G
open A (low)

1.
      C   E7   C   F
"**Take**/ up your\ cross," the/ Sa-vior said,
   G7   Am   G7   Am
"If you would my dis-ci-ple be;
   F   C   G7   C
De-ny your/-self\, the world\ for-sake,
   F   C   Dm   Am
And hum-bly fol-low af-ter me."

2.
      C   E7   C   F
Take/ up your\ cross, let/ not its weight
   G7   Am   G7   Am
Fill your weak spir-it with a-larm;
   F   C   G7   C
His strength shall/ bear\ your spir\-it up,
   F   C   Dm   Am
And brace your heart and nerve your arm.

3.
      C   E7   C   F
Take/ up your\ cross and/ fol-low Christ,
   G7   Am   G7   Am
Nor think til death to lay it down;
   F   C   G7   C
In faith-ful/ bear\-ing of\ our cross
   F   C   Dm   Am
We hope to wear his glo-rious crown.

4.
      C   E7   C   F
To/ you, great\ Lord, the/ One in Three,
   G7   Am   G7   Am
All praise for-ev-er-more as-cend:
   F   C   G7   C
O grant us/ in\ our home\ to see
   F   C   Dm   Am
The heav'n-ly life that knows no end.

58   LENT   HH Singer, pg 65

C 4/4
↓ _ ↓ ↑
4 r m i t
3 A C E G
open C

THE WORD OF GOD PROCEEDED FORTH

Text: Thomas Aquinas, d. 1274; translated, stanzas 1 & 4 by John M. Neale, d. 1866,
stanzas 2 & 3 by Gerard Manley Hopkins, d. 1889, altered
Music: OLD HUNDREDTH, LM, Louis Bourgeois, first published in Genevan Psalter, 1551
Popular Melody for: *Praise God From Whom All Blessings Flow*, page 120

1.
      C   Am   F   E7
The word of God, pro-ceed-ed forth
      C   Am   F   G7
Yet leav-ing not his Fa-ther's side,
    G6   E7   Am   C
And go-ing to his work on earth
    Am   F   G6   C   ↓
Had reached at length life's eve-ning tide.

2.
    •   Am   F   E7
Soon by his own false friend be-trayed,
    C   Am   F   G7
Giv-en to foes, to death he went;
    G6   E7   Am   C
His ve-ry self, in form of bread,
    Am   F   G6   C   ↓
Gi-ven to them, his friends he sent.

3.
    •   Am   F   E7
The man-ger, Christ their e-qual made;
    C   Am   F   G7
That up-per room, their soul's re-past;
    G6   E7   Am   C
The cross, their ran-som dear-ly paid,
    Am   F   G6   C   ↓
Heav-en, their high re-ward at last.

4.
    •   Am   F   E7
All praise and thanks to you as-cend
    C   Am   F   G7
For ev-er-more, blest one in three.
    G6   E7   Am   C
O grant us life that shall not end
    Am   F   G6   C   ↓
In our true na-tive land to be.

AT THE CROSS HER STATION KEEPING

Text: Jacopone da Todi, *Stabat Mater dolorosa*, d. 1306, translated by Edward Caswell, altered
Verse 3 by Stephen J. Wolf, 2011
Music: 88 7 STABAT MATER, *Mainz Gesanbbuch*, 1661

C 4/4
↓ _ ↓ ↑
4 r m i t
3 A C E G
open C

1.
    C   Am   •   F   C↓
At the cross, her sta-tion keep-ing,
   •   Am   F   Am   G7↓
Stood the mourn-ful moth-er weep-ing,
   •   E7   G7   C↓
Where he hung, the dy-ing Lord.

2.
   •   Am   •   F   C↓
Saw him then from judge-ment ta-ken,
   •   Am   F   Am   G7↓
And in death by all for-sa-ken,
   •   E7   G7   C↓
Till his Spir-it he re-signed.

3.
   •   Am   •   F   C↓
Sit with her this Sab-bath Ho-ly
   •   Am   F   Am   G7↓
Let our time with her be whole-ly
   •   E7   G7   C↓
Bless-ed in our grief to share.

4.
   •   Am   •   F   C↓
Je-sus, may her deep de-vo-tion
   •   Am   F   Am   G7↓
Stir in me the same e-mo-tion,
   •   E7   G7   C↓
Heart to heart ac-cep-tance find.

60 ALLELUIA! SING TO JESUS

EASTER — HH Singer, pg 86

3/4
↑_ ↑↓ ↑↓
or ↓ ↑ ↓
4 *t r i m*   Claw A↓ G
open C

Text: William C. Dix; *Altar Songs, Verses on the Holy Eucharist,* 1867, altered
Music: 87 87 D, HYFRYDOL, Rowland H. Prichard, 1811-1887
Popular melody for: *Love Divine, All Love Excelling,* page 112

1

```
C    Am      F     G7        C     Am     G7       C
```
Al-le-lu/-ia! sing to Je-\sus!   his the scep-ter, his\ the throne!
```
 •   Am      F     G7        C     Am     G7       C
```
Al-le-lu/-ia! his the tri\-umph,   his the vic-to-ry \ a-lone.
```
 •       Am       F     Dm        C     Am     Dm       G7
```
Hark! the songs\ of peace-ful Zi \-on   thun-der like/ a migh\-ty flood.
```
 C       Dm      C     G7        C     F      G7       C
```
Je\-sus out\ of ev\-'ry na//\-tion   has re-deemed\ us by his blood.

2

```
 •   Am      F     G7        C     Am     G7       C
```
Al-le-lu/-ia! not as or \-phans   are we left in sor\-row now;
```
 •   Am      F     G7        C     Am     G7       C
```
Al-le-lu/-ia! he is near\ us,   faith be-lieves, nor ques\-tions how;
```
 •       Am       F     Dm
```
Though the cloud\ from sight re-ceived\ him
```
    C       Am    Dm        G7
```
when the for/-ty days\ were o'er.
```
 C       Dm      C     G7
```
Shall\ our hearts\ for-get\ his pro//\-mise:
```
 C       F       G7       C
```
"I am with\ you ev-er-more?"

3

```
 •   Am      F     G7        C     Am     G7       C
```
Al-le-lu/-ia! King e-ter\-nal,   you the Lord we know as our own;
```
 •   Am      F     G7        C     Am     G7       C
```
Al-le-lu/-ia! Son of Ma\-ry,   earth your foot-stool, heav'n\ your throne:
```
 •       Am       F     Dm        C     Am     Dm       G7
```
In-ter-ces\-sor, Friend of sin\-ners, robed in flesh/ our great\ High Priest;
```
 C       Dm      C     G7        C     F      G7       C
```
You\ on earth\ both priest\ and vic//\-tim   in the Eu\-cha-ris-tic feast.

HH Singer, pg 84 — EASTER — 61

CHRIST THE LORD IS RIS'N TODAY

C 4/4
↑ _ ↑ ↓
4 *tr m i m*
3 A G E C
open C

Text: Charles Wesley, 1739, altered
Music marked: 77 77 LLANFAIR with alleluias, Robert Williams, d. 1821

1

    C   Am   G7   Dm   G7 Am Dm C
Christ the Lord is ris'n to\-day,   A \ \ -le \-lu-ia!
   •   Am   G7   Dm   G7 Am Dm C
Daugh-ters, sons and an-gels\ say,   A \ \ -le \-lu-ia!
 E7   G7   F   Dm   C • G7 •
Raise your joys and tri\-umphs\ high, A \ / -le-lu-ia!
   C   Am   G7   Dm   G7 Am Dm C
Sing, ye heav'ns, and earth, re\-ply,   A \ \ -le \-lu-ia!

2

   •   Am   G7   Dm   G7 Am Dm C
Lives a-gain our glo-rious\ King,   A \ \ -le \-lu-ia!
   •   Am   G7   Dm   G7 Am Dm C
Where, O Death, is now your\ sting,   A \ \ -le \-lu-ia!
 E7   G7   F   Dm   C • G7 •
Once he died our souls\ to\ save,   A \ / -le-lu-ia!
   C   Am   G7   Dm   G7 Am Dm C
Where your vic-to-ry, O\ Grave,   A \ \ -le \-lu-ia!

3

   •   Am   G7   Dm   G7 Am Dm C
Hail the Lord of earth and\ heav'n,   A \ \ -le \-lu-ia!
   •   Am   G7   Dm   G7 Am Dm C
Praise to God by both be\ giv'n!   A \ \ -le \-lu-ia!
 E7   G7   F   Dm   C • G7 •
Chil-dren of the Res-ur-rec\-tion,   A \ / -le-lu-ia!
   C   Am   G7   Dm   G7 Am Dm C
Our e-lec-tion has been\ won!   A \ \ -le \-lu-ia!

62   EASTER   HH Singer, pg 91

C 4/4
↓ _ ↓ ↑
4 r m i t
3 A G E C

CROWN HIM WITH MANY CROWNS
Text: From Revelation 19:12; Verses by Matthew Bridges, 1851, altered
Music: DIADEMATA, George J. Elvey, 1868

(for Easter)

open C   SLOWLY

① 1

```
     C              Am      F   •    C        F         G7         •
Crown him with ma-ny crowns     The Lamb up-on his throne;
         C       F        D          G7       Am     F      G7  •
Hark how the heav'n-ly an-them\ drowns All mu-sic but its own.
     C      G7       F   Am        F       G7       E7    G7
A-wake, my soul, and sing     Of him who died for thee
         C       F        G7    C          F      G7      C    •
And hail him as your King of kings  Through all e-ter-ni-ty.
```

② 2

```
     •          Am      F   •    C       F         G7         •
Crown him the Lord of Love.   Be-hold his hands and side,
         C      F       D         G7        Am     F    G7  •
Rich wounds, yet vis-i-ble a\-bove,  In beau-ty glo-ri-fied.
     C      G7       F   Am        F       G7       E7    G7
No an-gel in the sky      Can ful-ly bear that sight,
         C        F         G7         C        F     G7        C   •
But down-ward bends his wond'-ring eye At mys-te-ry so bright!
```

③ 3

```
     •          Am      F   •    C        F         G7        •
Crown him the Lord of Heav'n,  En-throned in worlds a-bove,
         C       F       D        G7
Crown him the King to whom is\ giv'n
     Am         F         G7      •
The won-drous name of Love.
         C       G7       F    Am         F         G7       E7  G7
Crown him with ma-ny crowns       As thrones be-fore him fall;
         C       F       G7       C        F      G7        C   •
Crown him, you kings, with ma-ny crowns For he is King of all.
```

HH Singer, pg 81   EASTER   63

FULL EASTER JOY THE DAY WAS BRIGHT

C
↓ ↑ ↓
4 *tr m i*
3 A E C A E G
Claw A ↓ G

open G (low)

Text: *Claro paschali gaudio,* 5th century unknown author,
tranlated by John M. Neale, 1851, 1861, altered
Music: PUER NOBIS NASCITUR, LM, Trier manuscript 15th C., Michael Praetorius, 1609

1

     C   Am   •   C
Full East-er joy, the day was bright,
    G7   •   C   •
Sun shin-ing out/ with fair-er light,
    F   G7   Am   G7
When to their long-ing eyes re-stored,
    C   G7   Am   C
His glad a-pos-tles saw their Lord.

2

     C   Am   •   C
He bade them see his hands, his side,
    G7   •   C   •
Where yet the glo/-rious wounds a-bide;
    F   G7   Am   G7
The to-kens true which made it plain
    C   G7   Am   C
Their Lord in-deed was ris'n a-gain.

3

     C   Am   •   C
The Christ, the King of gen-tle-ness,
    G7   •   C   •
Now you, your-self/, our hearts pos-sess
    F   G7   Am   G7
That we may give you all our days
    C   G7   Am   C
The trib-ute of our grate-ful praise.

64   EASTER   HH Singer, pg 77

AT THE LAMB's HIGH FEAST WE SING

C $\frac{4}{4}$
↓ _ ↓ ↑
4 *r m i t*
3 A G E C
open G

Text: Author unknown, 6th Century?, translated by Robert Campbell, 1849, altered
Music: 77 77 D, SALZBURG; Jakob Hintze, 1678; adapted by Johann Sebastian Bach, d. 1750
Popular melody for: *Songs of Thankfulness and Praise*, page 38

(1)

| C | G7 | • | C | G7 | F | Dm | C |

At the Lamb's high feast we sing, Praise to our vic-tor-ious King,

| • | G7 | • | C | G7 | F | Dm | C |

Who has washed us in the tide Flow-ing from his pier-ced side;

| G7 | G6 | C | G7 | F | C | E7 | Am |

Praise we him/, whose love div-ine Gives his sa-cred blood for wine,

| C | F | C | G7 | Am | F | G7 | C |

Gives his bod-y for the feast, Christ the Vic-tim, Christ the Priest.

(2)

| • | G7 | • | C |

Where the Pas-chal blood is poured,

| G7 | F | Dm | C |

Death's dark an-gel sheathes his sword;

| • | G7 | • | C |

Is-rael's hosts tri-um-phant go

| G7 | F | Dm | C |

Through the wave that drowns the foe.

| G7 | G6 | C | G7 |

Praise we Christ/, whose blood was shed,

| F | C | E7 | Am |

Pas-chal Vic-tim, Pas-chal Bread;

| C | F | C | G7 | Am | F | G7 | C |

With sin-cer-i-ty and love Eat we Man-na from a-bove.

(3)

| • | G7 | • | C | G7 | F | Dm | C |

Migh-ty Vic-tim from the sky, Hell's fierce pow'rs be-neath you lie;

| • | G7 | • | C | G7 | F | Dm | C |

You have o-pened Par-a-dise, That in you your saints may rise.

| G7 | G6 | C | G7 | F | C | E7 | Am |

Hymns of glo-/ry and of praise, Fa-ther now to you we raise;

| C | F | C | G7 | Am | F | G7 | C |

Ris-en Lord, all praise to thee, Ev-er with the Spir-it be.

HH Singer, pg 85 — EASTER — 65

HOLY FEAST YOU HOLY DAY

C 4/4
↓ _ ↓ ↑
4 r m i t
3 A G E C
open G

Text: Venantius Fortunatus, d. 609;
translated by Maurice F. Bell, *Hail Thee Festival Day*, 1906, altered
Music: 77 77 D, SALZBURG; Jakob Hintze, 1678; adapted by Johann Sebastian Bach, d. 1750
Popular melody for: *Songs of Thankfulness and Praise*, page 38

(for Easter)

①

    C   G7   •   C
Ho-ly Feast, you ho-ly day!
  G7   F   Dm   C
To be hal-lowed ev-er-more,
  •   G7   •   C
Day when Christ our Lord was raised,
  G7   F   Dm   C
Break-ing down the reign of death.
  G7   G6   C   G7
Praise the Giv/-er of all good!
  F   C   E7   Am
Con-cord Au-thor of all love,
  C   F   C   G7
Pour your balm on all our days;
  Am   F   G7   C
To your peace guide all our ways.

②

 • G7 •   C   G7   F   Dm   C
Lo, fair beau-ty of the earth, From the death of win-ter, rise!
 • G7 •   C   G7   F   Dm   C
With its Mas-ter now re-turns Ev'-ry good gift of the year.
G7 G6   C   G7   F   C   E7   Am
Ris-en from/ the grave, now Lord, Au-thor of cre-a-ted life,
    C   F   C   G7
Tread-ing through the path of death,
  Am   F   G7   C
New life to us all you give.

66 HOLY FEAST YOU HOLY DAY

EASTER — HH Singer, pg 92

C 4/4
↑ _ ↑ ↓
4 r m i t
3 A G E C
open G

Text: Venantius Fortunatus, d. 609;
translated by Maurice F. Bell, *Hail Thee Festival Day*, 1906, altered
Music: 77 77 D, SALZBURG; Jakob Hintze, 1678; adapted by Johann Sebastian Bach, d. 1750
Popular melody for: *Songs of Thankfulness and Praise*, page 38

(for Ascension)

③

| C | G7 | • | C | G7 | F | Dm | C |

Ho-ly Feast, you ho-ly day! To be hal-lowed ev-er-more,

| • | G7 | • | C | G7 | F | Dm | C |

Day when Christ our Ris-en Lord, Rose to hea-ven then to reign.

| G7 | G6 | C | G7 | F | C | E7 | Am |

He who to/ a cross was nailed, Now is ru-ler, Lord of all.

| C | F | C | G7 | Am | F | G7 | C |

All you crea-tures of the earth Sing the glo-ry of your God.

④

| • | G7 | • | C | G7 | F | Dm | C |

Dai-ly grows the love-li-ness Blos-somed glo-ry so a-dorned.

| • | G7 | • | C | G7 | F | Dm | C |

Gates of hea-ven o-pen wide Fling-ing her in-crease of light.

| G7 | G6 | C | G7 | F | C | E7 | Am |

Je-sus, heal/-er of the world, Light our minds, Re-deem-er great,

| C | F | C | G7 | Am | F | G7 | C |

One be-got-ten Son of God, Pray for us from God's right hand.

EASTER
67

HH Singer, pg 95

C 4/4
↑ _ ↑ ↓
4 *r m i t*
3 A G E C
open G

HOLY FEAST YOU HOLY DAY

Text: Venantius Fortunatus, d. 609;
translated by Maurice F. Bell, *Hail Thee Festival Day*, 1906, altered
Music: 77 77 D, SALZBURG; Jakob Hintze, 1678; adapted by Johann Sebastian Bach, d. 1750
Popular melody for: *Songs of Thankfulness and Praise*, page 38

(for Pentecost)

⑤

```
    C      G7       •     C    G7      F     Dm        C
Ho-ly Feast, you ho-ly day!  To be hal-lowed ev-er-more,
    •      G7       •     C    G7      F     Dm        C
Day the Ho-ly Spir-it came  Full of grace in-to the world.
    G7     G6       C     G7   F       C     E7        Am
Bright and shi/-ning like the fire On those wait-ing for the Lord,
    C      F        C     G7   Am            F     G7   C
Sud-den swift, the Spir-it fell,  Whom Christ Je-sus did fore-tell.
```

⑥

```
    •      G7       •     C    G7      F     Dm        C
From the Son and Fa-ther come  Sev'n-fold gifts of mys-ter-y
    •      G7       •     C    G7      F     Dm        C
Pour-ing on the hu-man soul  Rich-es in-fin-ite di-vine.
    G7     G6       C     G7   F       C     E7        Am
Ho-ly Spir-it of life and pow'r,  Flow in us, O sac-red font,
    C      F        C     G7   Am            F     G7   C
Light that light-ens up us all,  Breath of God's vo-ca-tion call.
```

68   EASTER   HH Singer, pg 79

JESUS CHRIST IS RIS'N TODAY

C 4/4
↓ ↑ ↓ ↑
4 r m i t
3 A C E G
open C

Text: Bohemian Carol, *Surrexit Christus hodie*, 1372, translated by John Walsh, 1708, stanzas 1-3 by John Arnold, 1749, stanza 4 by Charles Wesley, 1740, altered
Music: 77 77 EASTER HYMN with alleluias, *Lyra Davidica,* 1708

1
    C   G7   F   Am   C   F   G6 C
Je-sus **Christ** is ris'n to-day\,   A / / \ /-le /-lu \-ia!
   F   Am   F   G6   C   F   G6 C
Our tri-umph-ant ho-ly day\,   A / / \ /-le /-lu \-ia!
  G7   Dm   C   G6 G7   C   E7 G7
Who did once up-on the cross,   A / / \ /-le /-lu \-ia!
 •   C   F   Am   C   Am   G7   C
Suf/-fer\ to re-deem our loss\,   A \ / \ / /-le /-lu \-ia!

2
 •   G7   F   Am   C   F   G6   C
Hymns of praise, then, let us sing\,   A / / \ /-le /-lu \-ia!
  F   Am   F   G6   C   F   G6 C
Un-to Christ, our heav'n-ly King\,   A / / \ /-le /-lu \-ia!
  G7   Dm   C   G6 G7   C   E7 G7
Who en-dured the cross and grave,   A / / \ /-le /-lu \-ia!
 •   C   F   Am   C   Am   G7   C
Sin/-ners\ to re-deem and save\,   A \ / \ / /-le /-lu \-ia!

3
 •   G7   F   Am   C   F   G6   C
But the pain which he en-dured\,   A / / \ /-le /-lu \-ia!
  F   Am   F   G6   C   F   G6 C
Our sal-va-tion has pro-cured\,   A / / \ /-le /-lu \-ia!
  G7   Dm   C   G6 G7   C   E7 G7
Now a-bove the sky he's King,   A / / \ /-le /-lu \-ia!
 •   C   F   Am   C   Am   G7   C
Where/ the\ an-gels ev-er sing\,   A \ / \ / /-le /-lu \-ia!

4
 •   G7   F   Am   C   F   G6   C
Sing we to our God a-bove\,   A / / \ /-le /-lu \-ia!
  F   Am   F   G6   C   F   G6 C
Praise e-ter-nal as God's love\,   A / / \ /-le /-lu \-ia!
  G7   Dm   C   G6 G7   C   E7 G7
Praise God, all you heav'n-ly host,   A / / \ /-le /-lu \-ia!
 •   C   F   Am   C   Am   G7   C
Fa/-ther\, Son, and Ho-ly Ghost\,   A \ / \ / /-le /-lu \-ia!

EASTER 69

SING WITH ALL THE SAINTS IN GLORY

C 4/4
↓ ↑ _ ↑
4 r m i t
3 A G E C
open E

Text: 1 Corinthians 15:20, William J. Irons, *Psalms and Hymns*, 1873
Music: 8787D, HYMN TO JOY, Ludwig van Beethoven, 1770; adapted by Edward Hodges, 1827
Popular melody for: *Joyful Joyful We Adore You*, page 85

①
    C   F   G7   E7
Sing with all the saints in glo-ry,
  C   E7   Am   G7
Sing the res-ur-rec-tion song!
  C   F   G7   E7
Death and sor-row, earth's dark sto-ry,
  C   Dm   G7   C
To the for-mer days be-long.
  G7   C   G7   C
All a-round the clouds are/ break-ing,
  G7   E7   Am   G7
Soon the/ storms of time shall cease;
  C   F   G7   E7
In God's im-age we, a-wa-king,
  C   Dm   G7   C   ↓
Know the ev-er-last-ing peace.

②
  •   F   G7   E7
O what glo-ry, far ex-ceed-ing
  C   E7   Am   G7
All that eye has yet per-ceived!
  C   F   G7   E7
Ho-liest hearts, for a-ges plead-ing,
  C   Dm   G7   C
Nev-er that full joy con-ceived.
  G7   C   G7   C
God has prom-ised, Christ pre/-pares it,
  G7   E7   Am   G7
There on/ high our wel-come waits.
  C   F   G7   E7
Ev-'ry hum-ble spir-it shares it;
  C   Dm   G7   C   ↓
Christ has passed th'e-ter-nal gates.

70   EASTER   HH Singer, pg 78

THE DAY OF RESURRECTION

C 4/4
↓↑↓↑
4 tr m i m
3 A C E G A C E G
Claw A E ↓ G A E ↓ G
open E

Text: John of Damascus, d. 749,
translated from Greek by John M. Neale, 1862, altered
Music: 76 76 D, AURELIA, Samuel S. Wesley, 1864
Popular melody for: *The Church's One Foundation*, page 126

1

```
       C              Am             Dm              C
The day of Res-ur-rec-tion!  Earth, tell it out a-broad
      G7              Am             F              G7
The Pass-o-ver of glad-ness,  the Pass-o-ver of God.
      G6              Am             C              F
From death to life e-ter-nal,  from earth un-to the sky,
      E7              G7             F              C
Our Christ has brought us o-ver,  the vic-t'ry song on high.
```

2

```
                      Am             Dm              C
Our hearts be free of e-vil,  that we may see a-right
      G7              Am             F              G7
The Lord in rays e-ter-nal  of res-ur-rec-tion light;
      G6              Am             C              F
To lis-ten for his ac-cent,  may we be calm and plain,
      E7              G7             F              C
May his own greet-ing hear-ing,  we raise the vic-tor strain.
```

3

```
                      Am             Dm              C
Now let the heav'ns be joy-ful!  Let earth the song be-gin!
      G7              Am             F              G7
A-round the world keep tri-umph,  and all that is there-in!
      G6              Am             C              F
Let all things seen and un-seen  their notes in glad-ness blend
      E7              G7             F              C
For Christ the Lord has ris-en,  our joy that has no end.
```

THE HEAD THAT ONCE WAS CROWNED WITH THORNS

C 4/4
↓ ↑ _ ↑
4 r m i t
3 A C E G
open C
SLOWLY

Text: Thomas Kelly, *Hymns on Various Passages of Scripture,* 1820, altered
Music: MCKEE, CM; African American Spiritual, arr. by Harry T. Burleigh, d.1949
Popular melody for: *In Christ There Is No East or West*, page 102

1

```
              C         G7          C7           F
The/ Head that once was/ crowned with thorns
         Am       F      C      Am
Is crowned in glo\-ry/ now;
      E7    C     G6     C
A/ roy-al di-a-dem a-dorns
         E7      G7         C       G7
The/ migh/-ty vic\-tor's brow.
```

2

```
         C        G7         C7        F       Am       F       C Am
The/ high-est place that/ heav'n af-fords  Be-longs to him\ by/ right;
       E7    C       G6      C        E7      G7       C  G7
The/ King of kings and Lord of lords  and/ heav'ns/ e-ter\-nal Light.
```

3

```
         C       G7         C7        F      Am     F     C      Am
The/ joy of all who/ dwell a-bove,  The joy of all\ be/-low,
       E7    C      G6        C       E7       G7      C  G7
To/ whom he man-i-fests his love And/ grants/ his Name\ to know.
```

4

```
         C       G7         C7        F         Am      F      C Am
To/ them the cross with/ all its shame, With all its grace\, is/ giv'n;
       E7      C      G6      C        E7      G7       C   •
Their/ name an ev-er-last-ing name,  Their/ joy/ the joy\ of heav'n.
```

72   EASTER   HH Singer, pg 80

THE STRIFE IS O'ER

3/4
↓ ↑ ↓
4 *tr i m*
3 A E C A E G
Claw A ↓ G

open G

Text: from Psalm 98:1 by an unknown author, 1695,
translated by Francis Pott, 1859, altered
Music: 888 VICTORY with alleluias, Giovanni P. Da Palestrina, 1591,
adapted by William Monk, d.1889

1

   C   F   G7   C
The strife is o'er, the bat\-tle done;
   E7   Am   F   G7
Now is the vic-tor's tri\-umph won;
   C   F   G7   C
Now is the song of praise\ be-gun.
 •   G7 C ↓   •   G7 C ↓   G7   F G7 ↓   G6   E7 C ↓
Al-le-lu-ia!   Al-le-lu-ia!   Al-le-lu-ia!   Al-le-lu-ia!

2

   C   F   G7   C
Death's migh-tiest pow'rs have done\ their worst,
   E7   Am   F   G7
And Je-sus has his foes\ dis-persed;
   C   F   G7   C
Let shouts of praise and joy\ out-burst.
 •   G7 C ↓   •   G7 C ↓   G7   F G7 ↓   G6   E7 C ↓
Al-le-lu-ia!   Al-le-lu-ia!   Al-le-lu-ia!   Al-le-lu-ia!

3

   C   F   G7   C
On the third morn he rose\ a-gain
   E7   Am   F   G7
Glo-rious in maj-es-ty\ to reign;
   C   F   G7   C
Oh, let us swell the joy\-ful strain!
 •   G7 C ↓   •   G7 C ↓   G7   F G7 ↓   G6   E7 C ↓
Al-le-lu-ia!   Al-le-lu-ia!   Al-le-lu-ia!   Al-le-lu-ia!

HH Singer, pg 82   EASTER

YE SONS AND DAUGHTERS

⁶⁄₈
↓_ ↓ ↑ ↓_
4 tr m i
3 A E C A E G

Text: see John 20; attrib. to Jean Tisserand, d. 1494; translated by John M. Neal, 1851, altered
Music: 888, O FILII ET FILIAE; Chant Mode II, *Airs sur les hymnes sacrez, odes et noels*, 1623

open A (low)

①   F   C   G7   F
Ye sons and daugh\-ters of\ the King,
     •   C   G7   F
With heav'n-ly hosts\ in glo\-ry sing,
     •   Am   C   E7   G7   Am
To-day the grave\ has lost\ its sting: Al - le - lu - ia!

② F   C   G7   F   •   C   G7   F
On that first morn\-ing of\ the week, Be-fore the day\ be-gan\ to break,
     •   Am   C   E7   G7   Am
The Ma-rys went\ their Lord\ to seek: Al - le - lu - ia!

③ F   C   G7   F   •   C   G7   F
An an-gel bade\ their sor\-row flee, By speak-ing thus\ un-to\ the three:
     •   Am   C   E7   G7   Am
"Your Lord is gone\ to Gal\-i-lee:"   Al - le - lu - ia!

④ F   C   G7   F
That night th'A-pos\-tles met\ in fear,
     •   C   G7   F
A-midst them came\ their Lord\ most dear
     •   Am   C   E7   G7   Am
And said, "Peace be \ un-to\ you here:"   Al - le - lu - ia!

⑤ F   C   G7   F
Bless-ed are they\ that have\ not seen
     •   C   G7   F
And yet whose faith\ has con\-stant been,
     •   Am   C   E7   G7   Am
In life e-ter\-nal they\ shall reign: Al - le - lu - ia!

⑥ F   C   G7   F   •   C   G7   F
And we with ho\-ly Church\ u-nite, As ev-er-more\ is just\ and right,
     •   Am   C   E7   G7   Am
In glo-ry to \ the King\ of light: Al - le - lu - ia!

   Am   F   C   E7   G7   Am   ↓
Al-le-lu-ia\!   Al-le\-lu-ia!   Al-le-lu-ia!

74   PENTECOST   HH Singer, pg 96

COME CREATOR SPIRIT

↓ ↑ ↓ ← Text: verses 1-5 & 10-11 from the Latin by Rabanus Mauras, d. 856, *Veni Creator Spiritus*,
4 tr m i   with assistance from the literal translation © 2008 by Bard Suverkrop-IPA Source, LLC
3 AC E G   verses 6-9 from an *Easter Prayer for Vocations* by Stephen J. Wolf, 2011, 2017
  or A E C A E G   Music: VENI CREATOR SPIRITUS, LM; Mode VIII
open C

(1)

```
         C    Dm     F      • •          Dm     G7        •
     Come/, Cre\-a-tor_ \ Spir/-it,   Souls\ of yours, now\ vis/-it:
      F     Am        C       Dm       •
     Fill/ with grace \ from be-yond / na/-ture
      G7       C7      G7       C         •   ↓
     All/ these hearts\ that you have cre-a \-ted.
```

(2)

```
         C    Dm     F      • •          Dm      G7        •
Your/ name is the Com _-fort Par-a-clete,   The high-est gift of our giv-ing God,
  F      Am        C      Dm     •    G7   C7    G7     C    • ↓
Font/ of life a-fire, your lov-ing char-i-ty,  Font / of spir-it-u-al a\-noint\-ing.
```

(3)

```
             C    Dm     F      •
       You/ sev \-en-fold_ \ ho-ly gift,
              •      Dm      G7        •
        Fing-er of the right \ hand of God,
             F      Am        C       Dm       •
        You who were prom-ised du-ly by the Fa /-ther,
         G7      C7      G7       C        •   ↓
        En-rich our throats \ to speak words \ you want heard.
```

(4)

```
              C    Dm     F      •
       Kin-dle light in our minds _, your ho-ly light;
               •      Dm      G7        •
        Send and in-fuse in-to hearts your love.
             F      Am        C       Dm       •
        Hu-man weak-ness dwell-ing in hu-man bod /-ies
         G7      C7      G7       C        •   ↓
        Your pow-er streng-thens in-to per-pe-tu-i-ty.
```

(5)

```
         C    Dm     F      • •          Dm     G7         •
   Spir-it, drive a-way ev _-'ry en-mit-y   Bring-ing the peace ev-er-last-ing.
    F     Am      C      Dm    •  G7   C7    G7     C    • ↓
   With you, our faith-ful lead-er pro/-ceed\-ing May we a-void\ all harm/ and e\-vil.
```

PENTECOST 75

          C   Dm   F   •
⑥ **Spir**-**it**, **come** and fill all _ your faith-ful hearts,
     •   Dm   G7   •
Set fire in us your con-firm-ing love,
   F   Am   C   Dm   •
Send forth your Spir-it in-to all cre-a /-tion
 G7   C7   G7   C   • ↓
And / the face of the earth / you will re-new.

          C   Dm   F   •
⑦ **Give** us Wis-dom to seek _ the face of God,
     •   Dm   G7   •
Com-pre-hen-sion of bap-tis-mal grace,
   F   Am   C   Dm   •
Good Judg-ment to dis-cern Christ's call to free /-dom.
 G7   C7   G7   C   • ↓
Give us the grace \ to know / the Fa-ther's will.

⑧
     C   Dm   F   • •   Dm   G7   •
Give us Cour-age for our_ vo-ca-tion "yes!", Know-ledge of what Je-sus teach/-es,
 F   Am   C   Dm   • G7   C7   G7   C   •↓
Rev-er-ence for the ways of our good Fa/-ther; Give/ us Strength\ to do/ the will of God.

⑨
     C   Dm   F   • •   Dm   G7   •
Give us fear of the Lord_, that joy-ful awe, Our wit-ness giv'n to the Ris-en Son:
 F   Am   C   Dm   • G7   C7   G7   C   •↓
May it be pleas\-ing to the/ Fa/-ther And help you, Spir-it, re-new/ the face of earth.

           C   Dm   F   • ↓
⑩ **Through** you, Spir-it, may we_ hear Je-sus Christ,
     •   Dm   G7   •
And bet-ter know our \ Fa /-ther.
   F   Am   C   Dm   •
You, Lov-ing Spir-it of the Fa-ther and the Son,
 G7   C7   G7   C   • ↓
May / our trust be in you for all time to come.

      C   Dm   F   • •   Dm   G7   •
⑪ **Glo**-**ry** be to our God_ and Fa/-ther, And to his Son Res-u-rec/-ted,
 F   Am   C   Dm   •
And to their Ho-ly Breath, the Spir-it Com-fort-er,
 G7   C7   G7   C   •   •   C7 C ↓
For gen-er-a-tions and each gen-er-a \-tion.   A /\ -men /.

76   HH Singer, pg 32

A MIGHTY FORTRESS IS OUR GOD

C 4/4
↓ ↑ ↓ ↑
4 *r m i t*
3   A G E C
open G

Text: based on Psalm 46; Martin Luther, 1529;
translated by Frederick H. Hedge, d.1890, altered
Music: 87 87 66 66 7 EIN' FESTE BURG; Martin Luther, 1529

①

```
     G        D      G       D    •
A migh-ty for/-tress is\ our God,
     D7    •       C    G    •
The bul-wark nev-er fail\\-ing;
        •       D      G       D    •
Our help-er, God/, a-mid\ the flood
     D7    •       C    G    •
Of mor-tal ills pre-vail\\-ing:
        •         C        D   •          •    C       G    •
For still/ our an-cient\ foe    Does seek to work us woe;
        •         C        D   •          •    C       Am        E7   •
His craft and pow'r are great,   And armed with cru-el hate,
     D7    •       C    G    •
On earth is not his e\\-qual.
```

②

```
        •       D      G       D    •
Do we in our/ own strength\ con-fide?
     D7    •       C    G    •
Our stri-ving would be los\\-ing,
        •       D      G       D    •
Were not the Sa/-vior on\ our side,
     D7    •       C    G    •
The Son of God's own choos\\-ing:
        •         C        D   •          •    C       G    •
You ask/ who that may\ be?      Christ Je-sus, it is he;
        •         C        D   •          •    C       Am        E7   •
Lord Sab-a-oth, his name,       From age to age the same,
     D7    •       C    G    •
And he must win the bat\\-tle.
```

HH Singer, pg 130

AMAZING GRACE

3/4
↓_ ↓ ↑ ↓_
4 *t r i m* or *t m i r m i*
3 A E C A E G   or Claw A ↓ G

Text: John Newton, 1779
Music: NEW BRITAIN, CM, unknown; *Virginia Harmony*, 1831

open G (low)

SLOW

①   C   C7   F   C

A-**ma**-**zing**\ Grace! How sweet the sound

•   Am   G7   ↓

That saved a\ wretch like me.

C   C7   F   C

I once\ was\ lost, but now/ am\ found,

Am   G6   C   ↓

Was blind, but\ now I see.

②   •   C7   F   C

'Twas grace that\ taught my heart to fear,

•   Am   G7   ↓

And grace my\ fears re-lieved.

C   C7   F   C

How prec\-ious\ did that grace/ ap\-pear

Am   G6   C   ↓

The hour I\ first be-lieved.

③   •   C7   F   C

Through ma-ny\ dan-gers, toils, and snares,

•   Am   G7   ↓

I have al\-rea-dy come.

C   C7   F   C

'Tis grace\ hath\ brought me safe/ thus\ far,

Am   G6   C   ↓

And grace will\ lead me home.

④   •   C7   F   C

When we've been\ there ten thou-sand years,

•   Am   G7   ↓

Bright shi-ning\ as the sun,

C   C7   F   C

We've no\ less\ days to sing/ God's\ praise

Am   G6   C   ↓

Than when we'd\ first be-gun.

78

HH Singer, pg 120

$^3_2$ **ALL CREATURES OF OUR GOD AND KING**

↓_ ↓ ↑ ↓_   Text: Francis of Assisi, 1225; translated by William H. Draper,
4   tr i m tr i m   *Public School Hymn Book,* 1919, altered
3   A E C A E G   Music: LASST UNS ERFREUEN, LM with alleluias; *Geistliche Kirchengesange,* 1623
open C

      C   Am   G7
① **All** crea-tures of our God and King
      C   Am   G7   Am↓↓   F   G7
Lift up your voice and with us sing,   Al-le-lu-ia!
      Am   G7   C
You burn-ing sun with gold-en beam,
      Am   G7   C
You sil-ver moon with soft-er gleam!

           F↓ ↓G7 C   Am↓ ↓   F G7   F↓ ↓ G7 C   Am
REFRAIN   Al-le-lu-ia!   Al-le-lu-ia!   Al-le-lu-ia!
              (TWICE?)   (TWICE?)

      C   Am   G7
② **You** flow-ing wa-ter, pure and clear,
      C   Am   G7   Am↓↓   F   G7
Make mu-sic for your Lord to hear,   Al-le-lu-ia!
      Am   G7   C
You fire so mas-ter-ful and bright,
      Am   G7   C
Giv-ing the hu-man warmth and light.   **REFRAIN**

      C   Am   G7
③ **Dear** moth-er earth, who day by day
      C   Am   G7   Am↓↓   F   G7
Un-fold your bless-ings on our way,   Al-le-lu-ia!
      Am   G7   C
Flow-ers and fruits, all in you grown,
      Am   G7   C
And God's own glo-ry let be shone.   **REFRAIN**

```
         C              Am                    G7
④ You rush-ing winds that are so strong,
         C              Am                    G7      Am↓↓  F  G7
   You clouds that sail in heav'n a-long,    Al-le-lu-ia!
      Am            G7                C
   You ri-sing moon, in praise re-joice,
      Am            G7                C
   You lights of eve-ning, find a voice!
```

```
                F↓ ↓G7  C    Am↓ ↓  F  G7    F↓ ↓ G7  C       Am
REFRAIN         Al-le-lu-ia!  Al-le-lu-ia!   Al-le-lu -ia!
                  (TWICE?)      (TWICE?)
```

```
         C              Am                 G7
⑤ And you most kind and gen-tle death,
         C              Am                    G7      Am↓↓  F  G7
   Wait-ing to hush our la-test breath,    Al-le-lu-ia!
      Am            G7                C
   You lead to home the child of God,
      Am            G7                C
   As Christ our Lord the way has trod.                              REFRAIN
```

```
         C              Am                 G7
⑥ Let all things their Cre-a-tor bless,
         C              Am                    G7      Am↓↓  F  G7
   And wor-ship God in hum-ble-ness,    Al-le-lu-ia!
      Am            G7                      C
   Praise, praise the Fa-ther, praise the Son,
      Am            G7                C
   And praise the Spir-it, Three in One!                             REFRAIN
```

80 HH Singer, pg 31

GOD OUR REFUGE

³₂
↓_ ↓↑ ↓_ Text: Psalm 46, by Stephen J. Wolf, 2003, tribute to the priesthood of Joseph E. Wesley
4 tr i m tr i m Music: LASST UNS ERFREUEN, LM with alleluias; *Geistliche Kirchengesange*, 1623
3 A E C A E G Popular melody for: *All Creatures of Our God and King*, page 78
open C

❶
```
C            Am           G7       C           Am           G7
God, our/ ref \-uge and strength,  Ev-er/ pres-ent help in stress.
Am↓ ↓    F  G7   Am↓ ↓    F  G7
God is with us,     so  we fear not.
   Am          G7                  C      Am          G7              C
Though the\ earth and moun-tains shake, Deep of\ wa-ters foam and rage,
 F↓    ↓  G7 C    F↓ ↓  G7 C
Moun-tains tot-ter,  wa-ter surg-ing,
Am↓ ↓  F  G7   Am↓ ↓   F    G7     F↓  ↓  G7      C        Am
God of Ja-cob    is our strong-hold,   God is with - - us.
```

❷
```
C            Am           G7       C           Am           G7
Ho-ly/ dwell-ing of our God,  Stream-ing / riv-er glad-den there
Am↓ ↓    F  G7   Am↓ ↓    F  G7
 In the cit- y    of our ref-uge.
   Am          G7                 C      Am          G7               C
Na-tions\ rage and king-doms fall,   All earth\ trem-bles at the call,
 F↓   ↓  G7 C    F↓  ↓  G7 C
God will help at    break of new day,
Am↓ ↓  F  G7   Am↓ ↓   F    G7     F↓  ↓  G7      C        Am
God of Ja-cob    is our strong-hold,   God is with - - us.
```

❸
```
C            Am           G7       C           Am           G7
"Be still and know that I am God."   Come and/ see the works of God:
Am↓ ↓    F  G7   Am↓ ↓  F  G7
Stop-ping war in    ev- 'ry na-tion,
   Am          G7                 C      Am          G7               C
Break-ing\ weap-on, break-ing spear,  Burn-ing\ bow and ar-mor shield,
 F↓  ↓  G7 C     F↓  ↓  G7    C
Say-ing, "Be still,   know your God now,"
Am↓ ↓  F  G7   Am↓ ↓   F    G7     F↓  ↓  G7      C        •
God of Ja-cob    is our strong-hold,   God is with - - us.
```

HH Singer, pg 134

AS ABBA LOVES YOU

9/4
↓ ↑ ↓
4 r m ti
3 A E C A E G

open C

Text: from John 15, Stephen J. Wolf, 2007, 2017 tribute to the priesthood of Charley Giacosa
Music: BUNESSAN 5554 D, Scots Gaelic melody
Popular melody for: *Morning Has Broken*

1.
    C   • Dm G7   F C
As Ab-ba loves you, Je-sus you love us
  C6   Em Am G6   G7
Teach-ing us to a-bide in your love.
  C   F Dm C   Am D
In your com-mand to love one an-oth-er
  G7   C F G7   C
As you have loved us, call-ing us friends.

2.
    •   • Dm G7   F C
You are the vine and we are your branch-es;
  C6   Em Am G6   G7
Let Ab-ba prune us so we bear fruit,
  C   F Dm C   Am D
Your word re-mem-b'ring, lov-ing each oth-er
  G7   C F G7   C
As you have loved us, call-ing us friends.

3.
    •   • Dm G7   F C
No great-er love has one than to lay down
  C6   Em Am G6   G7
One's ver-y life for e-ven a friend.
  C   F Dm C   Am D
We you have cho-sen, lov-ing each oth-er
  G7   C F G7   C
As you have loved us, call-ing us friends.

4.
    •   • Dm G7   F C
We have been with you from the be-gin-ning
  C6   Em Am G6   G7
To tes-ti-fy in Spir-it and truth,
  C   F Dm C   Am D
In word and ac-tion, lov-ing each oth-er
  G7   C F G7   C •
As you have loved us, call-ing us friends.

82 HH Singer, pg 62

AT BREAK OF DAY

3/4

↓_ ↓ ↑ ↓_
4 tr i m tr i m
3 A E C A E G

open C

Text: Psalm 90, by Stephen J. Wolf, 2007, tribute to the priesthood of William Nolan
Music: 11 11 11 11, ST. DENIO, Welsh Melody, John Roberts, *Canaidau y Cyssagr*, 1839
Popular melody for: *Immortal, Invisible, God Only Wise*, see page 83

1.
    F   G7   C   Am
At break of day fill us with wis-dom of heart;
    F   G7   C   Am
Give fa-vor and make good the work of your art.
    C   G6   C   E7
A thou-sand years hu-man like one day to you,
    F   G7   E7   C   C7
Our ref-uge through each gen-er-a-tion, re-new.

2.
    F   G7   C   Am
Be-fore bring-ing forth world-ly moun-tains and earth,
    F   G7   C   Am
You are God e-ter-nal with no end or birth.
    C   G6   C   E7
There is some-where in us made sad when we learn
    F   G7   E7   C   C7
That we are dust and to this dust we re-turn.

3.
    F   G7   C   Am
Though sev-en-ty years be the sum of our days,
    F   G7   C   Am
Or more for the strong, e-ven eigh-ty, for praise,
    C   G6   C   E7
Like grass that sprouts green in the new mor-ning air
    F   G7   E7   C   C7
Years end like a sigh, ebb a-way, this we share.

4.
    F   G7   C   Am
So wis-en'd with trou-bles, may we com-pre-hend:
    F   G7   C   Am
You want us to sing a glad song when we can,
    C   G6   C   E7
So fill us with mer-cy for joy through the land;
    F   G7   E7   C
Give fa-vor and pros-per the work of our hands.

HH Singer, pg 136

ETERNAL INVISIBLE GOD ONLY WISE

3/4
↓_ ↓↑ ↓_   Text: based on 1 Tim 1:17; Walter C. Smith, *Hymns of Christ and the Christian Life,* 1876, altered
4 *tr i m*   Music: 11 11 11 11, ST. DENIO, Welsh Melody, John Roberts, *Canaidau y Cyssagr,* 1839
3 A E C A E G SLOWLY   Original Lyrics: *Immortal Invisible God Only Wise*
open C

        F   G7   C   Am

① **E-ter-nal**, in-vis-i-ble, God on-ly wise.
    F   G7   C   Am
In light in-ac-ces-si-ble hid from our eyes,
    C   G6   C   E7
Most bless-ed, most glo-rious, the An-cient of Days,
    F   G7   E7   C   C7
Your Son and your Spir-it, your great name we praise.

    F   G7   C   Am

② **Un-rest-ing**, un-hast-ing, and si-lent as light,
    F   G7   C   Am
Nor want-ing, nor wast-ing, you rule day and night;
    C   G6   C   E7
Your jus-tice like moun-tains high soar-ing a-bove
    F   G7   E7   C   C7
Your clouds, which are foun-tains of bless-ing and love.

    F   G7   C   Am

③ **Great** Fa-ther of glo-ry, Cre-a-tor of light,
    F   G7   C   Am
Your an-gels a-dor-ing and saints in your sight;
    C   G6   C   E7
Of all your rich gra-ces this grace, Lord, im-part:
    F   G7   E7   C   C7
Un-cov-er our fa-ces and make clean our heart.

    F   G7   C   Am

④ **All** prais-es we ren-der; Lord help us to see
    F   G7   C   Am
The splen-dor of light that is hid-den in thee,
    C   G6   C   E7
And so let your glo-ry, Al-migh-ty, your art
    F   G7   E7   C   •
Be told in the sto-ry of Christ to the heart.

84 HH Singer, pg 107

BLESSED BE

C ⁴/₄

↓ ↑ _ ↑   Text: Ephesians 1:3-14, Stephen J. Wolf, 2008, with gratitude to the Institute for Priestly Formation
4 tr m i m   Music: 8787D, HYMN TO JOY, Ludwig van Beethoven, d. 1827; adapted by Edward Hodges, 1824
3 A G E C   Popular melody for: *Joyful, Joyful, We Adore Thee*, page 85
open E

1

```
  C       F       G7      E7       C       E7      Am       G7
**Bles**-sed be the God and Fa-ther  of our Lord/ Je-sus Christ,
  C       F       G7      E7       C       Dm      G7       C
Who has blessed us in the Christ\, bless-ings in their Spir-it breath.
  G7      C       G7               C       G7      E7      Am       G7
As God chose us in the Mes-si-ah  be-fore/ found-ing sky or earth,
  C       F       G7      E7       C       Dm      G7       C    ↓
To be ho-ly, clean of blem-ish,   in God's eye: a-dop-tion worth.
```

2

```
  •       F       G7      E7       C       E7      Am       G7
**In** the Son we have re-demp-tion, God's for-give-ness of our sin,
  C       F       G7      E7       C       Dm      G7       C
By the rich-es of his grace\ lav-ished on us gath-ered in.
  G7      C       G7               C       G7      E7      Am       G7
Giv-ing wis-dom, know-ledge/, vis-ion, mys-t'ry/ of the Fa-ther's will,
  C       F       G7      E7       C       Dm      G7       C    ↓
Sum-ming up all things in Je-sus, fa-vored in the full-ness sent.
```

3

```
  •       F       G7      E7       C       E7      Am       G7
**In** our hear-ing of the gos-pel word of our sal-va \-tion,
  C       F       G7      E7       C       Dm      G7       C
One by one we too were cho-sen, joined as part-ners with the Son.
  G7      C       G7       C       G7      E7      Am       G7
By the prom-is'd Ho-ly/ Spir-it, signed and/ sealed as heirs of God,
  C       F       G7      E7       C       Dm      G7       C   ↓
God's pos-ses-sion, God's re-demp-tion, God's be-lov-ed, Ab-ba's own.
```

HH Singer, pg 127   **85**

C 4/4   **JOYFUL JOYFUL WE ADORE YOU**
↓↑_↑   4   *tr m i m*   Text: Henry Van Dyke, 1907, altered
3   A G E C   Music: 8787D, HYMN TO JOY, Ludwig van Beethoven, d. 1827; adapted by Edward Hodges, 1824

open E   C   F   G7   E7   C   E7   Am   G7
①   **Joy**-ful, joy-ful, we a-dore you,   God of glo-ry, Lord of love;
       C   F   G7   E7   C   Dm   G7   C
Hearts un-fold like flow'rs be-fore you, Op'n-ing to the sun a-bove.
   G7   C   G7   C   G7   E7   Am   G7
Melt the clouds of sin and/ sad-ness; Drive the/ dark of doubt a-way;
   C   F   G7   E7   C   Dm   G7   C   ↓
Giv-er of e-ter-nal glad-ness,   Fill us with the light of day.

              •   F   G7   E7
      ②   **All** your works with joy sur-round you,
            C   E7   Am   G7
        Earth and heav'n re-flect your rays,
            C   F   G7   E7
        Stars and an-gels sing a-round you,
            C   Dm   G7   C
        Cen-ter of un-bro-ken praise;
           G7   C   G7   C
        Field and for-est, vale and/ moun-tain,
           G7   E7   Am   G7
        Flow'-ry/ mea-dow, flash-ing sea,
           C   F   G7   E7
        Chant-ing bird and flow-ing foun-tain,
           C   Dm   G7   C   ↓
        Call us to re-joice in thee.

             •   F   G7   E7   C   E7   Am   G7
③   **You** are giv-ing and for-giv-ing, Ev-er bless-ing, ev-er blest,
       C   F   G7   E7   C   Dm   G7   C
Well-spring of the joy of liv-ing, O-cean depth of hap-py rest!
G7   C   G7   C   G7   E7   Am   G7
You our Fa-ther, Christ our/ bro-ther, All who/ live in love are thine;
   C   F   G7   E7   C   Dm   G7   C   ↓
Teach us how to love each oth-er, Ho-ly Spir-it, joy div-ine.

86 HH Singer, pg 109

BEAUTIFUL SAVIOR

4/4

↓ ↑ _ ↑
4 r m i t
3 A G E C

open C

Text: based on Psalm 45:2; author unknown, 1677; translated by Joseph A. Seiss, 1873, altered
Music: ST. ELIZABETH; Hoffman and Richter's *Schleisische Volkslieder*, 1842

1
    C • G7 C Am • F C
Beau-ti-ful Sa\-vior, King of Cre-a\-tion,
  G7 F G7 F Dm Am E7 G7
Son of\ Ma-ry\, Son of God!
  C Dm G7 F • G7 F C
Tru-ly I love\ you, Tru-ly I'll serve\ you,
  E7 G7 Am G7 C ↓
Light of my soul, my Joy, my Crown.

2
  • • G7 C Am • F C
Fair are the mea\-dows, Fair are the wood\-lands,
  G7 F G7 F Dm Am E7 G7
Robed in\ flow-ers of bloom-ing spring;
  C Dm G7 F • G7 F C
Je-sus is fair\-er, Je-sus is pur\-er;
  E7 G7 Am G7 C ↓
He makes our sad-dest spir-it sing.

3
  • • G7 C Am • F C
Fair is the sun\-shine, Fair is the moon\-light,
  G7 F G7 F Dm Am E7 G7
Bright are the spark-ling\ stars on high;
  C Dm G7 F • G7 F C
Je-sus shines bright\-er, Je-sus shines pur\-er,
  E7 G7 Am G7 C ↓
Than all the an-gels in the sky.

4
  • • G7 C Am • F C
Beau-ti-ful Sa\-vior, Lord of the na\-tions,
  G7 F G7 F Dm Am E7 G7
Full-y\ hu-man\, full-y God!
  C Dm G7 F • G7 F C
Praise, a-do-ra\-tion, Glo-ry and ho\-nor,
  E7 G7 Am G7 C ↓
Now and for-ev-er-more, our Lord!

HH Singer, pg 143

COME HOLY SPIRIT WHOEVER ONE

³⁄₄

↓ ↑ ↓
4 *tr m i*
   or *t m i r m i*
3 A E C A E G
open G (low)

Text: attributed to Ambrose of Milan, *Nunc Sancte nobis Spiritus*, d.397;
translated by John Henry Newman, *Tracts for the Times*, 1836, altered
Music: LAMBILLOTTE, LM; with repeat; Louis Lambillotte, SJ, 1796-1855
Popular melody for: *Come, Holy Ghost, Creator Blest...*

①
      C   F   G7   Am
Come, Ho-ly Spir-it, who ev-er One
  •   G7   Am   G7
Are with the Fa\-ther and/ the Son;
  C   F   G7   Am
Come, Ho-ly Spir_it, our souls pos-sess
  C   F   C   G7
With your full flood of\ ho-li-ness;
  C   F   G7   C
With your full flood of\ ho-li-ness.

②
  •   F   G7   Am
In will and deed_, by heart and tongue,
  •   G7   Am   G7
With all our pow-ers, your praise/ be sung;
  C   F   G7   Am
Light up in love_ our hu-man frame,
  C   F   C   G7
Till o-thers catch the\ liv-ing flame;
  C   F   G7   C
Till o-thers catch the\ liv-ing flame.

③
  •   F   G7   Am
Fa-ther Al-migh-ty, hear now our cry
  •   G7   Am   G7
Through Je-sus Christ\ our Lord/ most high,
  C   F   G7   Am
Who with the Ho-ly Spir-it and Thee
  C   F   C   G7
Do live and reign e\-ter-nal-ly;
  C   F   G7   C
Do live and reign e\-ter-nal-ly.

88 COMFORT COMFORT O MY PEOPLE

HH Singer, pg 112

C
↓↑↓ & ↓↑↓↑
4 *tr m i* & *r m i t*
3 A G E C & A G E C
open C

Text: based on Isaiah 40:1-8 for the Feast of John the Baptist,
Johann G. Olearius, 1611-1684, trans. by Catherine Winkworth, 1827-1878, alt.
Music: 87 87 77 88, GENEVA 42, Claude Goudimel, *Geneva Psalter,* 1551
Advent verses are on page 5 (verses 2 and 3).

1

   C   Am   F↓↑↓↑   G7↓↑↓↑
Com-fort, com-fort, O my peo-ple,
   C   Am   E7↓↑↓↑   C↓↑↓↑
Speak of peace, thus says our God;
   •   Am   F↓↑↓↑   G7↓↑↓↑
Com-fort those who sit in dark-ness,
   C   Am   E7↓↑↓↑   C↓↑↓↑
Mourn-ing un-der sor-row's load;
Am   G7   Am↓↑↓↑ G7↓↑↓↑ G7   Am   F↓↑↓↑   E7↓↑↓↑
Speak un-to Je-ru-sa-lem   Of the peace that waits for them;
C   F   C↓↑↓↑   Am↓↑↓↑ Am   F   G7↓↑↓↑   C↓↑↓↑ •
Tell her all her sins I cov-er,   And that war-fare now is o-ver.

2

       •   Am   F↓↑↓↑   G7↓↑↓↑
Yes, all sins our God will par-don,
      C   Am   E7↓↑↓↑   C↓↑↓↑
Blot-ting each con-fessed mis-deed;
      •   Am   F↓↑↓↑   G7↓↑↓↑
All that well de-served the an-ger
      C   Am   E7↓↑↓↑   C↓↑↓↑
God will no more see nor heed.
Am   G7   Am ↓↑↓↑   G7↓↑↓↑
We have suf-fered man-y days,
G7   Am   F↓↑↓↑   E7↓↑↓↑
Now our grief has passed a-way;
    C   F   C↓↑↓↑   Am↓↑↓↑
God will change our heav-y sad-ness
Am F   G7↓↑↓↑   C↓↑↓↑   •
In-to ev-er spring-ing glad-ness.

HH Singer, pg 111

CROWN HIM WITH MANY CROWNS

C 4/4
↓ _ ↓ ↑
4 r m i t
3 A G E C
open C
SLOWLY

Text: From Revelation 19:12; Verses by Matthew Bridges, 1851, altered
Music: DIADEMATA, George J. Elvey, 1868

(for Ordinary Time)

**① **

```
     C          Am       F  •    C       F       G7      •
Crown him with ma-ny crowns    The Lamb up-on his throne;
     C       F       D       G7       Am      F       G7     •
Hark how the heav'n-ly an-them\ drowns  All mu-sic but its own.
     C       G7      F   Am     F       G7      E7      G7
A-wake, my soul, and sing     Of him who died for thee
     C       F       G7      C        F      G7      C       •
And hail him as your King of kings  Through all e-ter-ni-ty.
```

**② **

```
       •         Am      F  •    C       F       G7      •
Crown him the Vir-gin's Son,   The God in-car-nate born,
         C       F       D       G7      Am      F       G7     •
Whose arm those crim-son tro-phies\ won Which now his brow a-dorn;
      C       G7      F   Am     F       G7      E7      G7
Fruit of the mys-tic rose,     As of that rose the stem;
        C       F       G7      C        F      G7      C       •
The root whence mer-cy ev-er flows,  The Babe of Beth-le-hem.
```

**③ **

```
       •         Am      F  •    C       F       G7      •
Crown him the Lord of Heav'n,   En-throned in worlds a-bove,
      C       F       D       G7       Am      F       G7     •
Crown him the King to whom is\ giv'n  The won-drous name of Love.
      C       G7      F   Am     F       G7      E7      G7
Crown him with ma-ny crowns     As thrones be-fore him fall;
      C       F       G7      C        F      G7      C       •
Crown him, you kings, with ma-ny crowns  For he is King of all.
```

89

90

HH Singer, pg 37

FACE TO FACE

C 4/4

↓↑↓↑ or ↓_↓↑
4 r m i t
3 A G E C
open A (low)

Text: Psalm 82, Stephen J. Wolf, 2007, tribute to the priesthood of James D. Niedergeses, ninth bishop of Nashville
Music: 87 87 87 PICARDY, *Chansons Populaires des Provinces de France,* 1860
Popular melody for: *Let All Mortal Flesh Keep Silence,* page 91

     F   C   Am • G6 •
(1) Face to face with all who would be "gods,"
  Am   F   Dm Am   C •
Our God ri-ses to judge-ment give:
    F   C   Am • G6 •
"How long will you judge with-out jus-tice?"
  Am   F   Dm Am   C •
Asks the One true God who\ lives,
  Am   F   G7 • Am   ↓↑ C   G7 •
"How long will you give   To those with pow'r and means
  C   F   G7 E7   Am •
All your fa-vor, judge-ment, and will?"

    F   C   Am • G6 •
(2) "You who would be "gods," seek-ing pow-er,
  Am   F   Dm Am   C •
Nei-ther know nor un-der\-stand,
    F   C   Am • G6 •
Wan-der-ing the land, walk in dark-ness,
  Am   F   Dm Am   C •
Shake the world's foun-da-tion a-round;
  Am   F   G7 • Am   ↓↑ C   G7 •
'gods' though you would be,   Off-spring of the Most High,
  C   F   G7 E7   Am •
Your lives, mor-tal prin-ces, will end."

    F   C   Am • G6 •
(3) If you would be God's judg-ing ser-vant,
  Am   F   Dm Am   C •
Ren-der jus-tice to God's own poor,
    F   C   Am • G6 •
Keep-ing safe from all who would harm them,
  Am   F   Dm Am   C •
Or-phan, wid-ow, strang-er at shore.
  Am   F   G7 • Am   ↓↑ C   G7 •
To the low-ly and   peo-ple af-flict\-ed
  C   F   G7 E7   Am •
Give their due of earth's fruit and store.

HH Singer, pg 139

LET ALL MORTAL FLESH KEEP SILENCE

C 4/4
↓ ↑ ↓ ↑
4 r m i t
3 A G E C
open A (low)

Text: *Liturgy of St. James,* 5th Century; translated from Greek by Gerard Moultrie, 1864
Music: 87 87 87 PICARDY, *Chansons Populaires des Provinces de France,* 1860

①
      F   C   Am • G6 •
Let all mor-tal flesh keep\ si-lence,
 Am   F   Dm Am C   •
And with fear and trem-bling\ stand;
      F   C   Am • G6 •
Pon-der noth-ing earth-ly\ mind-ed,
 Am   F   Dm Am C   •
For with bless-ing in his\ hand,
 Am   F   G7 • Am   ↓↑C G7 •
Christ our God to earth   de-scend / /\-eth,
  C   F   G7 E7 Am •
Our full hom-age to de/-mand.

②
F   C   Am • G6 • Am   F   Dm Am C   •
King of kings, yet born of\ Ma-ry, As of old on earth he\ stood,
F   C   Am • G6 • Am   F   Dm Am C   •
Lord of lords, in hu-man\ ves-ture, In the bo-dy and the\ blood;
Am   F   G7 • Am   ↓↑C G7 • C   F   G7 E7   Am •
He will give to all the faith/ /\-ful His own self for heav-en-ly food.

③
      F   C   Am • G6 •
Rank on rank the host of\ heav-en
 Am   F   Dm Am C   •
Spreads its van-guard on the\ Way,
      F   C   Am • G6 •
As the Light of light de\-scend-eth
 Am   F   Dm Am C   •
From the realms of end-less\ day,
 Am   F   G7 • Am   ↓↑C G7 •
That the pow'rs of hell   may van / /\-ish
  C   F   G7 E7 Am •
As the dark-ness clears a/-way.

92

HH Singer, pg 102

C $^4_4$

↓ _ ↓ ↑
4 r m i t
3 A C E G or A C E G A C E G
open C

FROM ALL THAT DWELL BELOW THE SKIES

see Psalm 117
Text: Isaac Watts, *The Psalms of David,* 1719;
Robert Spence, *Pocket Hymn Book,* 1780, altered
Music: DUKE STREET, LM; John Hatton, 1793

**① **

    C   G7   C   G7
From all that dwell be/-low the\ skies,
  •   Am   F   G7
Let the Cre-a-tor's praise a-rise;
G6   C   Am   Dm
Let the Re-deem/-er's/ Name\ be\ sung,
  G7   Am   G6   C
Through ev-'ry land, by ev-'ry tongue.

**② **

  •   G7   C   G7
E-ter-nal are your/ mer-cies\, Lord;
  •   Am   F   G7
E-ter-nal truth at-tends your Word.
 G6   C   Am   Dm
Your praise shall sound/ from/ shore\ to\ shore,
G7   Am   G6   C
Till suns shall rise and set no more.

**③ **

  •   G7   C   G7
In ev-'ry land be/-gin the\ song;
  •   Am   F   G7
To ev-'ry land the strains be-long;
G6   C   Am   Dm
In cheer-ful sounds/ all/ voi\-ces\ raise,
G7   Am   G6   C
And fill the world with loud-est praise.

HH Singer, pg 88

C 4/4
↓ _ ↓ ↑
4 *r m i t*
3 A G E C
open C

I KNOW THAT MY REDEEMER LIVES

Text: from Job 19:25-27, Samuel Medley, 1775, altered
Music: DUKE STREET, LM; John Hatton, 1793
Popular melody for: *From All That Dwells Below The Skies*, page 92

(1)
```
      C              G7        C            G7
I know that my Re/-deem-er\ lives;
      •              Am        F            G7
What com-fort this sweet sen-tence gives!
G6              C           Am          Dm
Liv-ing\ Proph/-et/, Priest\, and\ King;
G7           Am         G6         C
Liv-ing and as he lives I'll sing.
```

(2)
```
      •              G7        C            G7
He lives/ hun-gry/ souls to\ feed,
      •              Am        F            G7
Liv-ing to help in time of need.
G6              C           Am          Dm
Liv-ing to grant/ us/ rich\ sup\-ply,
G7           Am         G6         C
Liv-ing to guide us with his eye.
```

(3)
```
      •              G7        C            G7
He lives/ qui-et/ing our\ fears,
      •              Am        F            G7
Liv-ing to wipe a-way our tears,
G6              C           Am          Dm
Liv-ing to calm/ our/ troubl\-ed\ heart,
G7           Am         G6         C
Liv-ing all bless-ings to im-part.
```

(4)
```
      •              G7        C            G7
He lives/, glo-ry/ to his\ Name!
      •              Am        F            G7
Liv-ing, my Je-sus, still the same.
G6              C           Am          Dm
Oh, sweet the joy/ this/ sen\-tence\ gives:
G7           Am         G6         C
"I know that my Re-deem-er lives!"
```

94   HH Singer, pg 103

C 4/4   **FOR THE BEAUTY OF THE EARTH**

↓ _ ↓ ↑   4 tr m i m   Text: *Lyra Eucharistica*, 1864; Folliot S. Pierpoint, 1864, altered
3 A C E G   Music: 77 77 77, DIX, Conrad Kocher, 1838; adapt. by William H. Monk, 1823-99

```
open C   C           G7      F       C     Am      F      G7       C
      ① For the/ beau-ty of the earth,  For the glo-ry of the skies,
         •           G7      F       C     Am      F      G7       C
         For the/ love which from our birth  O-ver and a-round us lies.
         •       Am      G7        C     Am      F      G6        C   •
         Lord of all, to you we raise  This our song of grate-ful praise.

         •           G7      F       C     Am      F      G7       C
      ② For the/ beau-ty of each hour,  Of the day and of the night,
         •           G7      F       C     Am      F      G7       C
         Hill and/ val-ley, tree and flow'r,  Sun and moon and stars of light.
         •       Am      G7        C     Am      F      G6        C   •
         Lord of all, to you we raise  This our song of grate-ful praise.

         •           G7      F       C     Am      F      G7       C
      ③ For the/ joy of ear and eye,  For the heart and mind's de-light,
         •           G7      F       C     Am      F      G7       C
         For the/ mys-tic har-mo-ny  Link-ing sense to sound and sight.
         •       Am      G7        C     Am      F      G6        C   •
         Lord of all, to you we raise  This our song of grate-ful praise.

         •           G7      F       C     Am      F      G7       C
      ④ For the/ joy of hu-man love,  Broth-er, sis-ter, par-ent, child,
         •           G7      F       C     Am      F      G7       C
         Friends on/ earth and friends a-bove,  Sa-cred res-pite from the wild.
         •       Am      G7        C     Am      F      G6        C   •
         Lord of all, to you we raise  This our song of grate-ful praise.

         •           G7      F       C     Am      F      G7       C
      ⑤ For your/ peo-ple ev-er-more  Lift-ing ho-ly hands a-bove,
         •           G7      F       C     Am      F      G7       C
         Off-'ring/ up on ev-'ry shore  Faith and sac-ri-fic-ial love.
         •       Am      G7        C     Am      F      G6        C   •
         Lord of all, to you we raise  This our song of grate-ful praise.

         •           G7      F       C     Am      F      G7       C
      ⑥ Per-fect/ gift of pres-ence thine  Won-drous gift so free-ly giv'n,
         •           G7      F       C     Am      F      G7       C
         Grac-es/ hu-man and div-ine,  Peace on earth and joy in heav'n.
         •       Am      G7        C     Am      F      G6        C   •
         Lord of all, to you we raise  This our song of grate-ful praise.
```

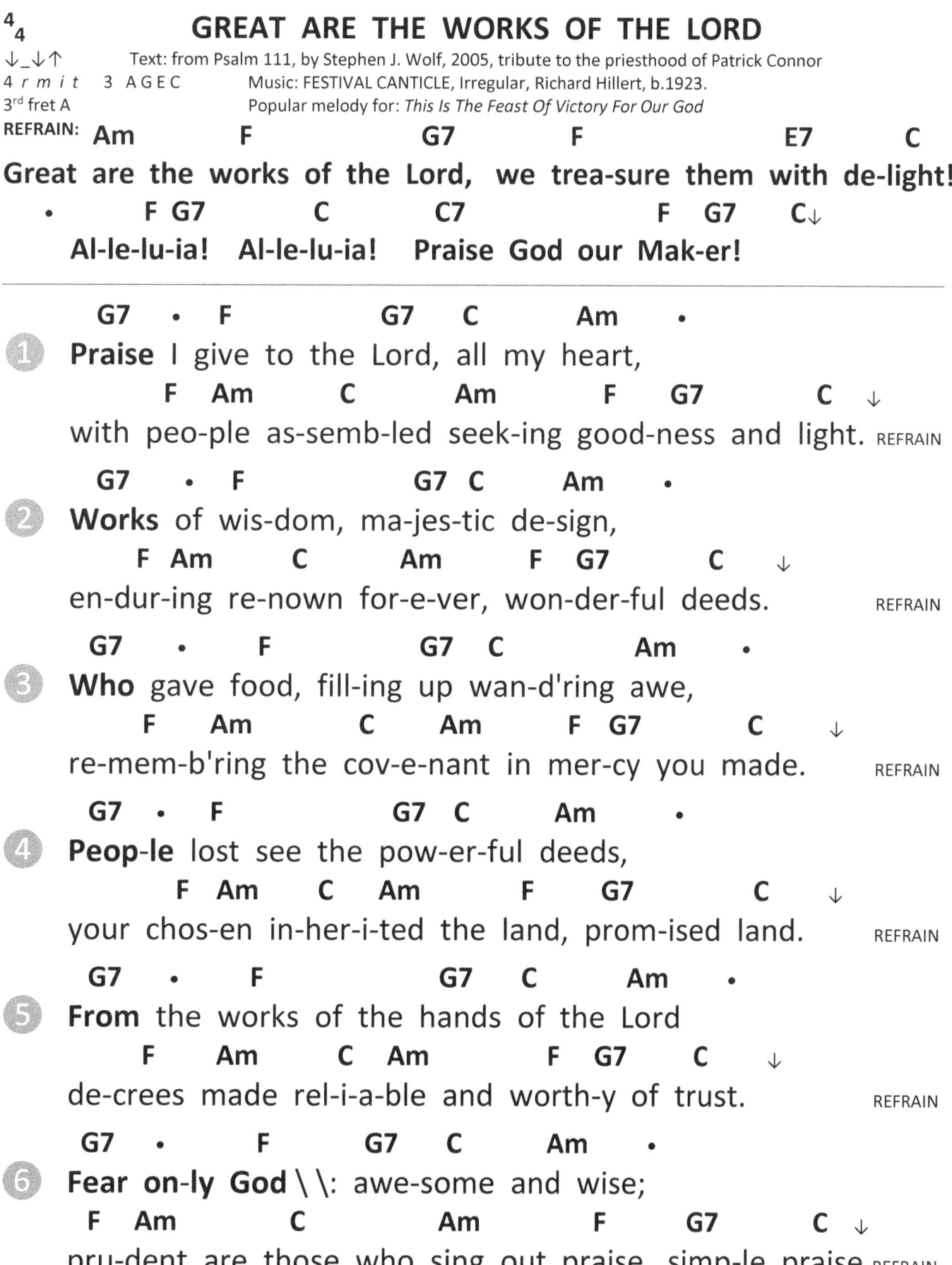

96 HH Singer, pg 142

HOLY GOD WE PRAISE YOUR NAME

³⁄₄
↓↑↓
4 tr m i

3 A E C A E G

open C

Text: Ignaz Franz, *Grosser Gott*, about 1774, translated by Clarence Walworth, 1858, altered
Music: 78 78 77 GROSSER GOTT, *Katholisches Gesangbuch, Vienna*, 1774

     C   Am   G7   C
① **Ho**-ly God\, we praise/ your Name;
   Am   F   G7   Am   G7↓
  Lord of all\, we bow\ be-fore you!
    C   Am   G7   C
  All on earth\ your scep/-ter claim,
   Am   F   G7   Am   G7↓
  All in heav-en a-bove\ a-dore you;
• F   C   G7   F   G7   F   C
In-fin/-ite\ your vast do/-main, Ev-er-last\-ing is\ your reign.

       •   Am   G7   C
② **Hark**! the loud\ cel-es/-tial hymn
   Am   F   G7   Am   G7↓
  An-gel choirs\ a-bove\ are rais-ing,
    C   Am   G7   C
  Cher-u-bim\ and ser/-a-phim,
   Am   F   G7   Am   G7↓
  In un-ceas\-ing chor\-us prais-ing;
• F   C   G7   F   G7   F   C
Fill the/ heav-ens with sweet ac/-cord: Ho-ly, ho\-ly, ho\-ly Lord.

       •   Am   G7   C
③ **Ho**-ly Fa\-ther, Ho/-ly Son,
   Am   F   G7   Am   G7↓
  Ho-ly Spir\-it, Three\ we name you;
    C   Am   G7   C
  While in ess\-ence on/-ly One,
   Am   F   G7   Am   G7↓
  Un-div-i\-ded God\ we claim you;
• F   C   G7   F   G7   F   C
And a/-dor\-ing bend the/ knee, While we en-ter the mys\-ter-y.

HH Singer, pg 114

HOLY HOLY HOLY

C 4/4
↓ _ ↓ ↑
4 *tr m i m*   3 A C E G
open C

Text: From Revelation 4:8; by Reginald Heber, 1827, altered
Music: 11 12 12 10, NICAEA; John B. Dykes, 1861

1)
    C   Am   G7 •   F •   C G6
Ho-ly, ho-ly, ho-ly, Lord God Al-migh-ty!
  G7 •   C G6   G7   Dm   G7   •
Ear-ly in the morn-ing our song shall rise to thee;
  C   Am   G7 •   F •   G7 •
Ho-ly, ho-ly, ho-ly, mer-ci-ful and migh-ty!
  C G7   F Am   F   G7   C   •
God in Three Per-sons, bless-ed Trin-i-ty!

2)
    • Am   G7 •   F •   C G6
Ho-ly, ho-ly, ho-ly! All the saints a-dore thee,
  G7 •   C G6   G7   Dm   G7   •
Cast-ing down their gold-en crowns a-round the glass-y sea;
  C   Am   G7 •   F •   G7 •
Cher-u-bim and ser-a-phim fall-ing down be-fore thee,
  C G7   F Am   F   G7   C   •
Who was, and is, and ev-er-more shall be.

3)
    • Am   G7 •   F •   C G6
Ho-ly, ho-ly, are you! Though con-fu-sion hide you,
  G7 •   C G6   G7   Dm   G7   •
Glo-ry shin-ing through the blurr of cloud-ed hu-man view;
  C   Am   G7 •   F •   G7 •
Ho-ly a-lone are you; there is none be-side you:
  C G7   F Am   F   G7   C   •
Per-fect and pure, your love in all you do.

4)
    • Am   G7 •   F •   C G6
Ho-ly, ho-ly, ho-ly! Lord_ God Al-migh-ty!
  G7 •   C G6   G7   Dm   G7   •
All cre-a-tion praise your name in earth and sky and sea.
  C   Am   G7 •   F •   G7 •
Ho-ly, ho-ly, ho-ly, mer-ci-ful and migh-ty!
  C G7   F Am   F   G7   C   •
God in Three Per-sons, bless-ed Trin-i-ty!

98 HH Singer, pg 152

HOW CAN I KEEP FROM SINGING

4/4
↓ ↑ _ ↑
4 r m i t
3 A C E G
open G (low)

Text: Robert Lowry, 1860, altered
Music: 87 87, ENDLESS SONG, Quaker Hymn; Robert Lowry, 1860

```
         C        E7      F       Dm       C           G7      Am      G7
① **My life flows on in end-less song**  A-bove earth's lam-en-ta-tion.
         C        E7      F       Dm       C     E7      F            C
   I hear that near and far-off hymn,   It hails a new cre-a-tion:
         G7        C         F         C        Am          F      Am       G7
   Thru all the tu-mult and the strife  I hear that mu-sic ring-ing;
         C     G7     Am      G6        C         Am       G7            C
   It finds an ech-o\ in my soul;   How can I keep from sing-ing?

              •        E7        F        Dm
② **What** though my joys and com-forts fade
              C         G7       Am       G7
   The Lord my Sa-vior liv-eth;
              C         E7       F        Dm
   What though the shad-ows gath-er round
              C         E7       F        C
   Songs in the night he giv-eth:
              G7        C         F        C
   No storm can shake my in-most calm,
              Am        F         Am       G7
   While to that ref-uge cling-ing;
              C         G7       Am       G6
   Since Christ is Lord of\ heav'n and earth,
              C         Am       G7       C
   How can I keep from sing-ing?

              •        E7        F        Dm       C         G7      Am      G7
③ **I lift** my eyes; the clouds grow thin;  I see the blue a-bove it;
         C        E7      F       Dm       C     E7      F            C
   And day by day clears way the path  Since first I learned to love it:
              G7        C         F        C         Am          F      Am       G7
   The peace of Christ makes fresh my heart, A foun-tain ev-er spring-ing;
              C     G7     Am      G6        C         Am       G7            C
   All things are mine since\ I am his;  How can I keep from sing-ing?
```

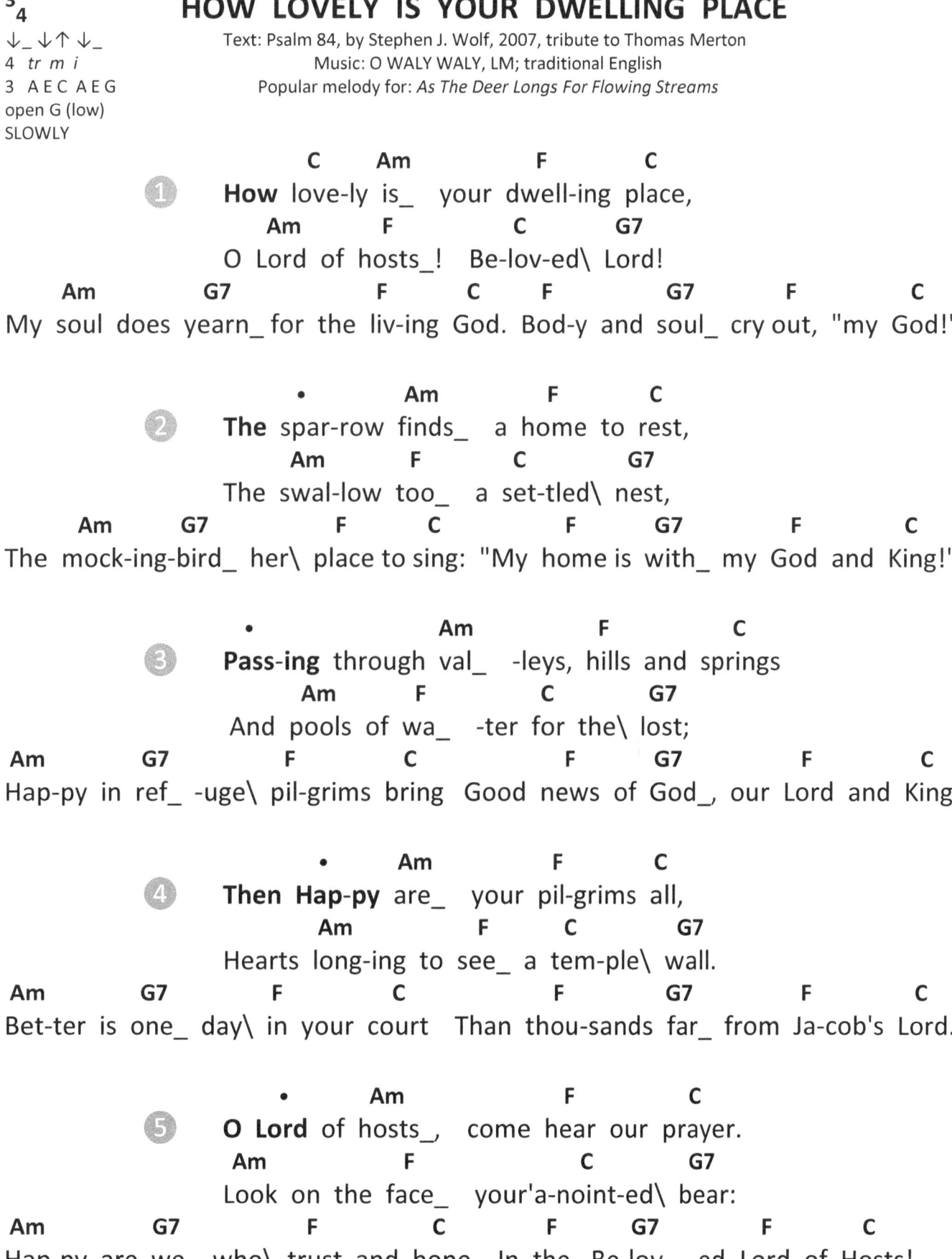

100 I HEARD THE VOICE OF JESUS SAY

HH Singer, pg 153

C 4/4
↓ ↑ _ ↑
4 *tr m i m*
3 A C E G
open C

Text: Horatius Bonar, *Hymns Original and Selected,* 1846, altered
Music: KINGSFOLD, CMD, traditional English melody,
adapted by Ralph Vaughan Williams, 1906

1

```
     F      Am    C    G7         C    Dm      G7   •
I\ heard the voice of Je-sus say,  "Come/ un-to me\ and rest;
     F      Am    C    G7
Lay\ down, you wea-ry one, lay down
         C    Dm     Am     •
Your/ head up-on\ my breast."
 G7      C      F   Am       C     F       G7   •
I/ came to Je\-sus as I was,  So/ wea-ry\, worn and sad;
     F      Am    C    G7        C    Dm    Am   ↓
I\ found in him a rest-ing place, And/ he has made\ me glad.
```

2

```
     F      Am    C    G7         C    Dm      G7   •
I\ heard the voice of Je-sus say,  "Be/-hold, I free\-ly give
     F      Am    C    G7         C    Dm    Am   •
The\ liv-ing wa-ter; thirs-ty one, Stoop/ down, and drink\ and live."
 G7      C      F   Am        C     F       G7   •
I/ came to Je\-sus, and I drank  Of/ that life\-giv-ing stream.
     F      Am        C    G7         C    Dm    Am   ↓
My\ thirst was quenched, my soul re-vived, And/ now I live\ in him.
```

3

```
     F      Am    C    G7        C    Dm      G7   •
I\ heard the voice of Je-sus say, "I/ am this dark\ world's light;
     F      Am    C    G7            C    Dm    Am   •
Look\ un-to me, your morn shall rise And/ all your day\ be bright."
 G7      C      F   Am         C     F       G7   •
I/ looked to Je\-sus, and I found  In/ him my\ star, my sun;
     F      Am    C    G7            C    Dm    Am   ↓
And\ in that light of life I'll walk, Till/ trav'l-ing days\ are done.
```

HH Singer, pg 117

I SING THE MIGHTY POW'R OF GOD

C 4/4
↓ ↑ ↓ ↑
4 r m i t
3 A G E C
open G (low)

Text: Isaac Watts, *Divine and Moral Songs for Children,* 1715
Music: 76 76 D, ELLACOMBE; *Gesangbuch der Herzogl,* Wirtemberg, 1784

①

    C   G7   C   G7   Am   G7   E7 ↓
I sing the\ migh-ty pow'r of God,   that made/ the moun-tains rise,
    C   G7   C   G7   Am   F   C ↓
That spread the\ flow-ing seas a-broad,   and built/ the loft-y skies.
 Am   •   G7   •   Am   •   G7 ↓
I/ sing the wis-dom that or/-dained   the/ sun to rule the day;
    C   G7   C   G7   Am   F   C ↓
The moon shines\ full at God's com-mand, and all/ the stars o-bey.

②

    •   G7   C   G7   Am   G7   E7 ↓
I sing the\ good-ness of the Lord, who filled/ the earth with food,
    C   G7   C   G7
Who formed the\ crea-tures through the Word,
 Am   F   C ↓
and then/ pro-nounced them good.
 Am   •   G7   •
Lord/, how your won-ders are dis/-played,
 Am   •   G7 ↓
  wher/-e'er I turn my eye,
    C   G7   C   G7   Am   F   C ↓
If I sur\-vey the ground or tread,   or gaze/ up-on the sky.

③

    •   G7   C   G7   Am   G7   E7 ↓
There's not a\ plant or flow'r be-low, but makes/ your glo-ries known,
    C   G7   C   G7   Am   F   C ↓
And clouds a\-rise, and temp-ests blow, by or/-der of your throne;
 Am   •   G7   •   Am   •   G7 ↓
While/ all that bor-rows life from/ you is/ ev-er in your care;
    C   G7   C   G7   Am   F   C ↓
And ev-'ry\-where that we can be, you, God/, are pres-ent there.

102 HH Singer, pg 147

C 4/4

↓ ↑ _ ↑
4 r m i t
3 A C E G
open C

IN CHRIST THERE IS NO EAST OR WEST

see Galatians 3:8

Text: William A. Dunkerley, 1908, under the pseudonym of John Oxenham, altered
Music: MCKEE, CM; African American Spiritual, arranged by Harry T. Burleigh, 1866-1949

       C   G7   C7   F

① In/ Christ there is no/ East or West,

   Am   F   C   Am

In him no South\ or/ North;

   E7   C   G6   C

But/ one com-mu-nion of God's love

   E7   G7   C   G7

Through/-out/ the whole\ wide earth.

       C   G7   C7   F

② In/ Christ shall true hearts/ ev-'ry-where

   Am   F   C   Am

Their high vo-ca\-tion/ find;

   E7   C   G6   C

His/ ser-vice is the gold-en cord,

   E7   G7   C   G7

Close/ bind/-ing hu\-man-kind.

       C   G7   C7   F

③ Join/ hands, then, mem-bers/ of the faith,

   Am   F   C   Am

What-e'r your race\ may/ be!

   E7   C   G6   C

Who/ serves my Fa-ther as his child

   E7   G7   C   G7

Is/ sure/-ly kin\ to me.

       C   G7   C7   F

④ In/ Christ now meet both/ East and West,

   Am   F   C   Am

In him meet South\ and/ North;

   E7   C   G6   C

All/ souls of Christ are one in him

   E7   G7   C   •

Through/-out/ the whole\ wide earth.

HH Singer, pg 154   103

JERUSALEM MY HAPPY HOME

6/4
↓ ↑ ↓
4 tr m i
3 A E C A E G
open G (low)

Text: F.B.P., London, around 1583, altered
Music: C.M., 86 86, LAND OF REST, traditional American melody

**① **

```
   C     G7         F      G7           C      G7    Em    •
Je-ru-sa-lem/, my hap-py home\, When shall I come/ to thee?
         F     Am        C      G6        Am      F       C   ↓
When shall my sor-rows have an end\? Your joys when shall\ I see?
```

**② **

```
    •    G7         F      G7         C      G7    Em  •
The saints are crowned/ with glo-ry great\; They see God face/ to face;
       F     Am         C      G6        Am      F      C   ↓
They tri-umph still/, they still re-joice\, No grief or wor-ry their case.
```

**③ **

```
    •    G7         F      G7           C      G7    Em   •
King Da-vid stands/, his harp in hand\ As lea-der of/ the choir:
       F     Am          C      G6       Am      F      C   ↓
Ten thou-sand times/ that we be blessed\, That we his mu\-sic hear.
```

**④ **

```
    •    G7         F      G7           C      G7    Em   •
Our La-dy sings/ Mag-ni-fi-cat\ With tune sur-pass/-ing sweet,
       F     Am         C      G6        Am      F      C   ↓
And all the vir-/gins bear their part\, While sit-ting at\ her feet.
```

**⑤ **

```
    •    G7         F      G7           C      G7    Em   •
And Mag-da-len/ has left her grief\, With cheer-ful joy/ does sing
       F     Am         C      G6        Am      F      C   ↓
And bless-ed saints/, their har-mo-ny\ to ev-'ry room\ they bring.
```

**⑥ **

```
    •    G7         F      G7           C      G7    Em   •
Je-ru-sa-lem/, Je-ru-sa-lem\, God grant that I/ may see
       F     Am         C      G6        Am      F      C   ↓
Your end-less joy/, and of the same\ Par-ta-ker al\-ways be.
```

104 HH Singer, pg 90

JESUS MY LORD MY GOD MY ALL

3/4

↓_ ↓ ↑ ↓_
4 tr m i
3 A E C A E G

open G

Text: Henry A. Collins, 1854, altered; vs. 3 Frederick W. Faber, d. 1863, altered
Music: SWEET SACRAMENT, LM with refrain, *Romischkatholisches Gesanguchlein*, 1826

1

```
     C           Am       G7      F       Am              F       G7       C
Je-sus, my Lord\, my God/, my all\;   How late, my Je-sus, have I sought.
 •           Am       G7       F       Am             F       G7        C
You pour down rich\-es of/ your grace\;   How can I love you as I ought?
                    G7         F      G7       C
          Je-sus, our Lord, we you a-dore!
                    G7         F      G7       F
          Call us to love you more/ and more\.
                 Am         F      G7       C
          Call us to love you more and more.
```

2

```
 •           Am       G7       F      Am              F       G7       C
Je-sus, what could you have found/ in me\ That you have dealt so pa-tient-ly?
 •           Am       G7       F
How great the joy\ that you/ have brought\,
Am        F       G7        C
So far ex-ceed-ing hope or thought!
                    G7         F      G7       C
          Je-sus, our Lord, we you a-dore!
                    G7         F      G7       F
          Call us to love you more/ and more\.
                 Am         F      G7       C
          Call us to love you more and more.
```

3

```
 •           Am       G7      F      Am             F       G7       C
Had I but Ma\-ry's sin/-less heart\  With which to love you, dear-est King;
 •           Am       G7      F      Am             F       G7       C
O! with what bursts\ of fer/-vent praise\ Your good-ness, Je-sus, would I sing.
                    G7         F      G7       C
          Sweet Sac-ra-ment, we you a-dore!
                    G7         F      G7       F
          Call us to love you more/ and more\.
                 Am         F      G7       C
          Call us to love you more and more.
```

HH Singer, pg 123

105

LET GLORY BE TO GOD ON HIGH

4/4

↓ ↑ _ ↑ ↓ ↑ _ ↑
4 tr m i m tr m i m
3 A C E G A C E G
open A (low)

Text: *Gloria in excelsis Deo,* 8th C manuscript of the Liturgy of St. James;
translator unknown, 1858, altered
Music: VENI EMMANUEL, LM with refrain; 15th C.; adapt. by Thomas Helmore, 1856
Popular melody for: *O Come, O Come Emmanuel,* page 12

①   Am   G7   Am
Let glo-ry be to God/\ on high:
    C   G7   Am
And peace be on the earth as in the sky;
    F   C   G7
Good will to all! We bow\ the knee,
    Am   G7   Am
We praise, we bless, we wor/\-ship thee;
    G7   Am   G7   Am
We give you thanks, your Name/\ we sing,
    C   E7   Am   ↓
Al-migh-ty Father! Hea\\-v'nly King!

②   •   G7   Am
O Lord, the sole be-got/\-ten Son,
    C   G7   Am
Who bore the crimes the hu-man race had done;
    F   C   G7
The Fa-ther's Son, the Liv\-ing Word
    Am   G7   Am
Who takes a-way the sins/ of the world;
    G7   Am   G7   Am
O Lamb of God, whose ve-ry blood was spilt
    C   E7   Am   ↓
For all the world, and all\\ its guilt.

③   •   G7   Am
Have mer-cy on us, through/\ your blood;
    C   G7   Am
Re-ceive our prayer, O Lamb\\ of God!
    F   C   G7
For you are ho-ly, you\ a-lone,
    Am   G7   Am
At God's right hand, up-on/\ the throne.
    G7   Am   G7   Am
O Trin-i-ty, now be/\ a-dored,
    C   E7   Am   ↓
With you, O Ho-ly Spir-it, One\ Lord.

106 HH Singer, pg 137

LORD WHEN AT YOUR LAST SUPPER

C 4/4
↓ ↑ _ ↑
4 r m i t
3 A C E G
open E

Text: William H. Turton, 1859-1938, *Lord Who At Thy First Eucharist*, altered
Music: 10 10 10 10 10 10 UNDE ET MEMORES, William H. Monk, 1823-1899

①
      C   F   Am   C   G7 •
Lord, when at your Last Sup-per you did pray
   •   F   Am   C   E7 •
That all your Church might be for-ev-er one.
C F Am C G6 • Am   • G7   E7 G7 •
Grant us at ev'-ry Eu-cha-rist to say With long-ing heart and soul, "Your will be done."
C F Am C G7 •   F   Am   C G7 C •
O may we all one bread, one bod-y be, Through this blest Sac-ra-ment of U-ni-ty.

②
   • F Am C G7 •   • F Am C E7 •
For all your Church, O Lord, we in-ter-cede; Make all our sad div-is-ions soon to cease;
C F Am C G6 • Am   • G7 E7 G7 •
Draw us the near-er each, to each we plead, By draw-ing all to you, O Prince of Peace;
C F Am C G7 •   F   Am   C G7 C •
Thus may we all one bread, one bod-y be, Through this blest Sac-ra-ment of U-ni-ty.

③
   • F Am C G7 •
We pray for all who wan-der from your fold;
   • F Am C E7 •
O bring them home, Good Shep-herd of the sheep,
C F Am C G6 •
Back to the faith which saints be-lieved of old,
Am • G7 E7 G7 •
Back to the Church which still the faith does keep;
C F Am C G7 •
Soon may we all one bread, one bod-y be,
F Am C G7 C •
Through this blest Sac-ra-ment of U-ni-ty.

④
   • F Am C G7 •
So, Lord, at length when sac-ra-ments shall cease,
   • F Am C E7 •
May we be one with all your Church a-bove,
C F Am C G6 •
One with your saints in one un-bro-ken peace,
Am • G7 E7 G7 •
One with your saints in one un-bound-ed love;
C F Am C G7 •
More bless-ed still in peace and love to be
F Am C G7 C •
One with the Trin-i-ty in U-ni-ty.

HH Singer, pg 93

C 4/4
↓ ↑ _ ↑
4 r m i t
3 A C E G
open E

OPEN THE ANCIENT PORTALS

Text: Psalm 24, by Stephen J. Wolf, 2007, tribute to the priesthood of Allan J. Cunningham
Music: 10 10 10 10 10 10 UNDE ET MEMORES, William H. Monk, 1823-1899
Popular melody for: *Lord Who At The First Eucharist Did Pray*

      C   F   Am   C   G7 •
① **Earth** is the Lord's, and all that she con-tains;
   •   F   Am   C   E7 •
Built by the Lord o'er seas and riv-er rains.
   C   F   Am   C   G6 •
Who is the king of glo-ry, migh-ty One?
   Am   •   G7   E7   G7 •
The King of glo-ry is the Lord of hosts.
   C   F   Am   C   G7 •
The King of glo-ry en-ters by the Word.
     F   Am   C   G7   C •
O-pen the an-cient por-tals of the Lord;

   •   F   Am   C   G7 •
② **Who** may go up the moun-tain of the Lord?
   •   F   Am   C   E7 •
The clean of hand with pu-ri-ty of heart.
   C   F   Am   C   G6 •
They are the ones who seek the face of God
   Am   •   G7   E7   G7 •
Who save by jus-tice ev-'ry ho-ly place.
   C   F   Am   C   G7 •
Who is the king of glo-ry, migh-ty One?
     F   Am   C   G7   C •
The king of glo-ry is the Migh-ty Lord.

   •   F   Am   C   G7 •
③ **O-pen the an-cient por-tals** of the Lord;
   •   F   Am   C   E7 •
The King of glo-ry en-ters by the Word.
   C   F   Am   C   G6 •
Lift high, you gates, rise up you an-cient doors;
   Am   •   G7   E7   G7 •
Wel-come your king and lov-ers of the Lord.
   C   F   Am   C   G7 •
Who is the king of glo-ry, migh-ty One?
     F   Am   C   G7   C •
The king of glo-ry is Lord Sa-ba-oth.

LORD OF ALL BEING THRONED AFAR

108
HH Singer, pg 132

↓ ↑ ↓
4 *tr m i*
3 A E C A E G
open E

Text: Oliver Wendell Holmes, 1809-1894
Music: JESU DULCIS MEMORIA, LM; Model 1
Popular melody for: *O Radiant Light, O Sun Divine*

1
   C   Am   F   Am
Lord of all be-ing, throned a-far,
   C   G7   Em   C
Your glo-ry flames from sun and star;
  Am   F   C   D
Cen-ter and soul of ev-'ry sphere\\,
  Am   G7   E7   C   Am
And yet to lov-ing hearts how near.

2
   C   Am   F   Am
Sun of our life, your liv-ing ray
   C   G7   Em   C
Sheds on our path the glow of day;
  Am   F   C   D
Star of our hope, your gen-tle light\\
  Am   G7   E7   C   Am
Shall ev-er cheer the long-est night.

3
   C   Am   F   Am
Lord of all life, be-low, a-bove,
   C   G7   Em   C
Whose light is truth, whose warmth is love;
  Am   F   C   D
Be-fore the bril-liance of your throne\\
  Am   G7   E7   C   Am
We ask no lus-ter of our own.

4
   C   Am   F   Am
Give us your grace to make us true,
   C   G7   Em   C
And kind-ling hearts that burn for you,
  Am   F   C   D
Till all your liv-ing al-tars claim\\
  Am   G7   E7   C   •
One ho-ly light, one heav'n-ly flame.

TO YOU WE OWE OUR HYMN OF PRAISE

↓ ↑ ↓
4 *tr i m*
3 A E C A E G
① open E

Text: Psalm 65, by Stephen J. Wolf, 2003, tribute to the priesthood of George Rohling
Music: JESU DULCIS MEMORIA, LM; Popular melody for: *O Radiant Light, O Sun Divine*

```
         C        Am        F      Am       C           G         Em        C
To you we owe our hymn of praise, Bur-dened with sin your peo-ples come.
                  Am          F         C        D
         You hear our prayer, O God of Zi\-on;
                  Am          G7        E7        C       ↓
②       Vows kept and bro-ken, made a-new.
 •            Am        F      Am       C           G         Em        C
Still ov-er-come are we by sin,  Lord you a-lone can par-don them.
                  Am         F        C         D
         Hap-py the cho-sen ones you bring with-in
                  Am          G7        E7        C       ↓
③       Your tem-ple court with good things giv'n.
 •            Am        F      Am       C           G         Em        C
You an-swer us with awe-some deed, Jus-tice and hope to ends of earth.
                  Am          F         C        D
         You still the roar-ing of the wave and sea;
                  Am          G7        E7        C       ↓
④       Set up the moun-tains by your might.
 •            Am        F      Am       C           G         Em        C
You still the tu-mult of the crowd, Now east and west re-sound with joy.
                  Am         F        C         D
         Peo-ple in lands and is-lands far a-way,
                  Am          G7        E7        C       ↓
⑤       See-ing your mar-vel stand in awe.
 •            Am        F      Am       C           G         Em        C
You vis-it earth and wa-ter her,  Ma-king a-bun-dant streams of life.
                  Am         F        C         D
         God's fer-tile earth pre-pared is blessed in rain,
                  Am          G7        E7        C       ↓
⑥       God's world sup-plied for fields of grain.
 •            Am        F      Am       C           G         Em        C
Lord, you are hope for all the earth,  You hear the hum-ble sing your praise.
                  Am         F        C         D
         Choose us a-gain, pour out your Spir-it free;
                  Am          G7        E7        C       •
         Bear fruit in us that all may see.
```

110 HH Singer, pg 101

LORD YOUR ALMIGHTY WORD (Let There Be Light)

$\frac{3}{4}$
↓_ ↓ ↑ ↓_
4 tr m i
3 A E C A E G
open G

Text: Based on Genesis 1:3, *Thou Whose Almighty Word*, John Marriott, 1813, altered
Music: 664 6664, ITALIAN HYMN (MOSCOW), Felice de Giardini, 1769

(1)
```
       C              G7          C
```
Lord, your al-migh\-ty Word
```
   •           F      G7      C           G6
```
Cha-os and dark/\-ness heard, And took their flight;
```
   G7           Am            G7          Am
```
Hear us we hum-bly pray, And where the gos-pel day
```
   C           G7           F           C↓
```
Sheds not its glo-rious ray, **Let there be light!**

(2)
```
   •           G7          C
```
Sa-vior, you came\ to give
```
   •           F      G7      C           G6
```
Those who in shad/\-ows live Heal-ing and sight,
```
   G7           Am            G7          Am
```
Health to the sick in mind, Sight to the in-ly blind,
```
   C           G7           F           C↓
```
Now to all hu-man-kind **Let there be light!**

(3)
```
   •           G7          C
```
Spir-it of truth\ and love,
```
   •           F      G7      C           G6
```
Life-giv-ing, ho/\-ly dove, Speed forth your flight!
```
   G7           Am            G7          Am
```
Move on the wa-ter's face Bear-ing the lamp of grace,
```
   C           G7           F           C↓
```
And in earth's sad-dest place, **Let there be light!**

(4)
```
   •           G7          C
```
Ho-ly and bless\-ed Three,
```
   •           F      G7      C           G6
```
Glo/-rious Trin/\-i-ty, Wis-dom, love, might;
```
   G7           Am            G7          Am
```
Bound-less as o-cean tide, Roll-ing in full-est pride,
```
   C           G7           F           C↓
```
Through the world far and wide, **Let there be light!**

HH Singer, pg 99

111

C 4/4

↓ _ ↓ ↑
4 tr m i m
3 A C E G
Claw A C ↓ G
open G

NOW THANK WE ALL OUR GOD

see Ecclesiastes 50:22-24
Text: Martin Rinckart, 1636, translation by Catherine Winkworth, 1858, altered
Music: 67 67 66 66, NUN DANKET; Johann Cruger, 1648

```
        G7        F       G7     •
Now thank we all our God
        F         G7      Dm  C    G6
With heart and hands and voi-ces,
        G7        F       G7     •
Who won-drous things has done,
        F         G7      Dm  C    G7
In whom this world re-joi-ces;
        •         C       G7     •
Who from our mo-thers' arms
        C         F       G7     •
Has blessed/ us on our way
        F         Dm      F      •
With count-less gifts of love,
        Dm        F       C      •
And still is ours to-day.
```

②

```
        G7        F       G7   •    F     G7    Dm  C   G6
All praise and thanks to God    Our Ab-ba now be giv-en,
        G7        F       G7   •    F     G7    Dm  C   G7
With Son and Spir-it as    They reign in high-est heav-en:
        •         C       G7   •    C     F     G7      •
The one e-ter-nal God,    Whom heav-en and earth a-dore!
        F         Dm      F    •    Dm    F     C   G6  C
For thus it was, is now,   And shall be ev-er-more.
```

112

HH Singer, pg 115

LOVE DIVINE ALL LOVE EXCELLING

3/4
↓ ↑ ↓
4 *tr i m*   3 A E C A E G
open C

Text: from Psalm 106:4; by Charles Wesley, 1747, altered
Music: 87 87 D, HYFRYDOL, Rowland H. Prichard, 1811-1887

①

```
    C        Am       F     G7        C        Am         G7          C
Love Div-ine/, all love ex-cell\-ing, Joy of heav'n, to earth\ come down,
   •    Am       F       G7         C         Am        G7          C
   Fix in us/ your hum-ble dwell\-ing, All your faith-ful mer\-cies crown.
   •    Am      F       Dm         C        Am       Dm        G7
   Je-sus, you\ are true com-pass\-ion,  Pure, un-bound/-ed love\ you are;
    C     Dm       C       G7         C      F       G7        C
   Vis\-it us\ with your\ sal-va//\-tion,  En-ter-ing\ the tremb-ling heart.
```

②
```
         •       Am           F      G7
   Breathe, oh breathe/, your lov-ing Spir\-it
         C    Am       G7          C
         In-to ev-'ry troub\-led breast;
         •    Am      F      G7
         Let us all/ in you in-her\-it,
         C        Am       G7         C
         Let us find the prom\-ised rest.
         •     Am        F         Dm
         Take a-way\ the love of sin\-ning;
         C      Am    Dm       G7
         Al-pha and/ O-me\-ga be;
         C       Dm     C       G7
         End\ of faith\ as its be-gin//\-ning,
         C          F      G7        C
         Set our hearts\ at lib-er-ty.
```

③
```
     •      Am        F      G7         C        Am        G7         C
   Fin-ish, then/, your new cre-a\-tion; Pure and spot-less let\ us be.
     •    Am       F       G7            C        Am         G7           C
     Let us see/ your great sal-va\-tion  Per-fect-ly re-stored\ and free,
     •    Am        F       Dm         C       Am       Dm        G7
     Changed from glo\-ry in-to glo\-ry,  Till in heav'n/ we find\ our place,
      C     Dm      C        G7            C     F       G7           C
     Till\ we cast\ our cares\ be-fore//\ you,  Lost in won\-der, love, and grace.
```

FR STEVE'S THREE-FINGER-CHORD UKULELE HYMNS, 2019

PROPHETS OUT OF ANCIENT TIMES

3/4
↑_ ↑↓ ↑_
4 t r i m
3 A E C A E G
open C

Text: Zech 7:9-10 & Mt 25, Stephen J. Wolf, 2017, tribute to the priesthood of Michael Johnston
Music: 87 87 D, HYFRYDOL; Rowland Prichard, 1811-1887
Popular melody for: *Love Divine, All Love Excelling*, page 112

1
```
     C         Am      F        G7        C         Am     G7       C
Proph-ets out/ of  an-cient times\  to  Je-sus out of Naz\-a-reth
 •         Am        F         G7        C         Am     G7           C
and his saints by the  Ho-ly Spir\-it    tell truth to we peo-ple of wealth:
            •        Am        F        Dm
         If we want to live  by our Lord's\ Way
              C          Am         Dm          G7
         we will watch for the mar-gin-al-ized.
              C         Dm         C         G7
         Their\ wel-fare\ is our\ best mea/-sure\ of
              C          F          G7           C
         our o-be-dience to God's de-signs.
```

2
```
     •         Am        F         G7        C         Am      G7         C
Judge with hum-ble and faith-ful jus\-tice know-ing who is Judge of us all
 •         Am       F         G7        C         Am      G7          C
for your Lord/ a- lone knows ev-'ry thought  in the heart of each of us all.
            •        Am        F         Dm
         To each o-ther show  kind com-pass\-ion
              C         Am         Dm         G7
         as to wid-ows and or-phans, the poor,
              C          Dm         C         G7
         with\ the res-i-dent strang\-er liv-ing in your midst;
              C           F          G7         C
         keep your heart clean of self-ish store.
```

3
```
 •         Am       F         G7        C         Am       G7         C
I was hung/-ry  so you fed\ me,  thirst-y and you gave me to drink,
 •         Am        F         G7        C         Am      G7           C
a-lien strang/-er and you wel-comed me, nak-ed and you gave me to wear,
 •         Am        F         Dm         C         Am       Dm         G7
sick so\ you  gave me tend-er care,  locked in pris-on, you vis-it-ed there;
  C          Dm         C         G7
when\ my peo-ple were griev-ing you bur/-ied their dead;
  C          F          G7         C
   Christ your King is for you pre-pared.
```

114   HH Singer, pg 67

³⁄₄   **THERE's A WIDENESS IN GOD's MERCY**
↓ ↑ ↓   Text: Frederick W. Fabor, 1814, 1863, altered
4 *tr i m* or *t i mr*   Music: 87 87 D, HYFRYDOL; Rowland Prichard, 1811-1887
3 A E C A E G   Popular melody for: *Love Divine, All Love Excelling*, page 112
open C

```
                                            ①
SLOWLY              C         Am        F          G7
              There's a wide/-ness in God's mer\-cy
                    C         Am        G7         C
              Like the wide-ness of\ the sea;
                    •         Am        F          G7
              There's a kind/-ness in God's jus\-tice
                    C         Am        G7         C
              Which is more than lib\-er-ty.
                    •         Am        F          Dm
              There is plen\-ti-ful re-demp\-tion
                    C         Am        Dm         G7
              In the blood/ that has\ been shed;
                    C         Dm        C          G7
              There\ is joy\ for all\ the mem//\-bers
                    C         F         G7         C
              In the sor\-rows of the Head.
                                            ②
      •     Am        F       G7        C        Am        G7        C
For the love/ of God is broad\-er  Than the meas-ures of\ our mind,
      •     Am        F       G7        C        Am        G7        C
And the heart/ of the E-ter\-nal  Be-yond won-der-ful\ and kind.
      •     Am        F       Dm        C        Am        Dm        G7
If our love\ were but more simp\-le  We might take/ him at\ his word,
      C     Dm        C       G7        C        F         G7        C
And\ our lives\ would be\ thanks-giv//\-ing  For the good\-ness of the Lord.
                                            ③
      •     Am        F       G7        C        Am        G7        C
Troub-led souls/, why will you scat\-ter  Like a crowd of fright\-ened sheep?
      •     Am        F       G7        C        Am        G7        C
Fool-ish hearts/, why will you wan\-der  From a love so true\ and deep?
      •     Am        F       Dm        C        Am        Dm        G7
There is wel\-come for the sin\-ner  And good gra/-ces for\ the good;
      C     Dm        C       G7        C        F         G7        C
There\ is mer\-cy with\ the Sa//\-vior,  There is heal\-ing in his food.
```

HH Singer, pg 122

O GOD OUR HELP IN AGES PAST

C 4/4
↓ ↑ _ ↑
4 *tr m i m*
3 A C E G
open C

Text: from Psalm 90:1,2,4, Isaac Watts, *The Psalms of David,* 1719, altered
Music: C.M., 86 86, ST. ANNE, William Croft, 1708

      F   C   F   Dm   F   Dm   C G7
① **O God**, our help in a-ges past, Our hope for years to come,
    F   G7   F   E7   Dm   G6   F   C
   Our shel-ter from the storm-y blast, And our e-ter-nal home.

      F   C   F   Dm
② **Be**-neath the shad-ow of your throne
    F   Dm   C   G7
   Your saints have dwelt se-cure;
    F   G7   F   E7   Dm   G6   F   C
   Suf-fic-ient is your arm a-lone, And our de-fense is sure.

      F   C   F   Dm   F   Dm   C G7
③ **Be-fore** the hills in or-der stood, Or earth re-ceived her frame,
    F   G7   F   E7   Dm   G6   F   C
   From ev-er-last-ing you are God, To end-less years the same.

      F   C   F   Dm   F   Dm   C G7
④ **A thou-sand** a-ges in your sight Are like an eve-ning gone;
    F   G7   F   E7   Dm   G6   F C
   Short as the watch that ends the night Be-fore the ri-sing sun.

      F   C   F   Dm   F   Dm   C G7
⑤ **Time**, like an ev-er-flow-ing stream, Bears all our lives a-way;
    F   G7   F   E7   Dm   G6   F   C
   They fly, for-got-ten, as a dream Dies at the op'n-ing day.

      F   C   F   Dm   F   Dm   C G7
⑥ **O God**, our help in a-ges past, Our hope for years to come,
    F   G7   F   E7   Dm   G6   F
   Be now our guard while trou-bles last, And our e-ter-nal home.

116

HH Singer, pg 150

O BREATHE ON ME O BREATH OF GOD

3/4

↓_ ↓↑ ↓_
4 tr m i tr m i
3 A E C A E G
open C

Text: Edwin Hatch, 1878, altered
Music: ST. COLUMBA, CM; Gaelic Folk Melody
Popular melody for: *The King Of Love My Shepherd Is*, page 117

1

```
     Am      G7      Am        C        Am      G7       C  C7
O/ breathe on me, O/ breath of God,  Fill/ me with life a//-new,
     F       G7       C        Am       G7      Am        C  •
That I may love what you have loved, And do what you would do.
```

2

```
     Am      G7      Am        C        Am      G7       C  C7
O/ breathe on me, O/ breath of God,  Un/-til my heart is// pure,
     F       G7       C        Am       G7      Am        C  •
Un-til with you I will one will,  To do and to en-dure.
```

3

```
     Am      G7      Am        C        Am      G7       C  C7
O/ breathe on me, O/ breath of God,  In/-spire my bu-sy// mind,
     F       G7       C        Am       G7      Am        C  •
Un-til this earth-ly part of me  Glows with your fire div-ine.
```

4

```
     Am      G7      Am        C        Am      G7       C  C7
O/ breathe on me, O/ breath of God,  My/ soul shall nev-er// die,
     F       G7       C        Am       G7      Am        C  •
But live in your e-ter-nal life,  Your love the rea-son why.
```

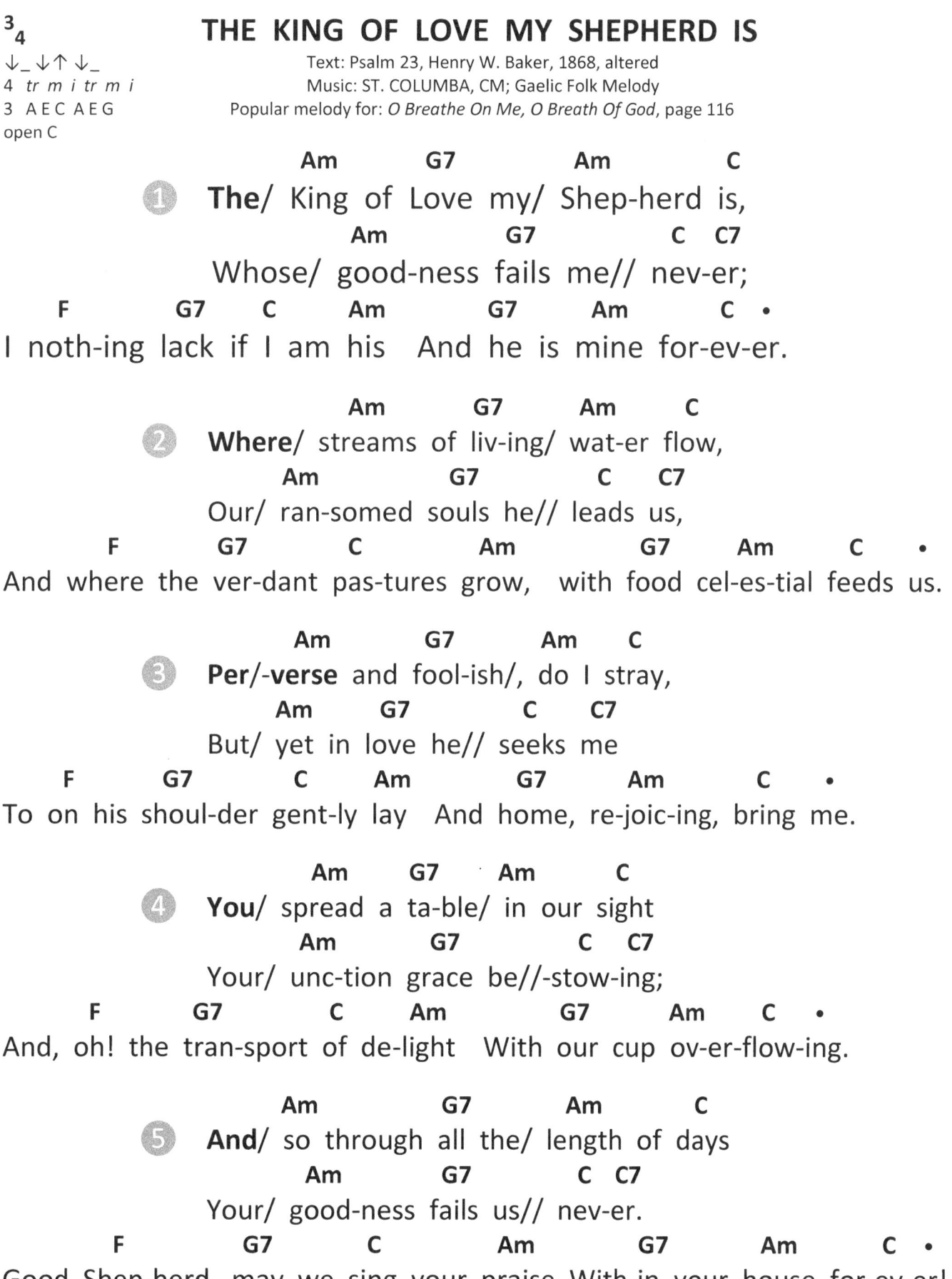

118   HH Singer, pg 133

O LORD OF LIFE

C ⁴₄
↓ _ ↓ ↑
4 *r m i t*
3 A C E G
open G (low)

Text: Washington Gladden, 1897, altered
Music: 86 86 86 86 FOREST GREEN, trad. English melody, harmony by Ralph Vaughan Williams, 1906
Popular melody used by James Quinn, SJ, in 1969 for the Morning Prayer *Canticle of Zechariah*

1.
    C   C7   Am   G7
O Lord of life, to you\ we/ lift
    F   G7   C   •
our hearts in\ praise for those,
    •   C7   Am   G7
Your proph-ets who have shown\ your/ gift
    F   G7   C   •
of grace that\ ev-er grows,
    G7   C   Am   G7
Of/ mer-cy spread\ from/ shore/ to/ shore,
    C   G7   E7   •
of wis-dom's wide-ning ray,
    C   F   G7   C
Of light that shines forth more\ and/ more
    F   G7   C   •
un-to your\ pro-mised day.

2.
    •   C7   Am   G7
Shine forth, O Light, that we\ may/ see,
    F   G7   C   •
with hearts made\ un-a-fraid,
    •   C7   Am   G7
The mean-ing and the mys\-te/-ry
    F   G7   C   •
of all that\ you have made:
    G7   C   Am   G7
O/ Light of light\! with\-in/ us/ dwell,
    C   G7   E7   •
through us your ra-diance pour;
    C   F   G7   C
Your truth be told in words\ and/ lives
    F   G7   C   •
that praise you\ ev-er-more.

HH Singer, pg 100

ON THIS DAY THE FIRST OF DAYS

C
↓ _ ↓ ↑
4 tr m i m
3 A C E G
open C

Text: *Le Mans Breviary,* 1748, *Hymns Ancient and Modern,* Henry W. Baker, 1861, altered
Music: 77 77 LUBECK, 77 77, *Gesanbuch* by Johann A. Freylinghausen, 1704

1

    C   G7   F   C
On this day, the first of days,
  G7   Dm   Am   G7
God the Fa-ther's Name we praise;
Am   G7   Dm   F
Who, cre-a-tion's Lord and Spring
Am   G7   Dm   C
Did the world from dark-ness bring.

2

•   G7   F   C   G7   Dm   Am   G7
On this day th'e-ter-nal Son Ov-er death has tri-umph won;
Am   G7   Dm   F   Am   G7   Dm   C
On this day the Spir-it came Bring-ing gifts of liv-ing flame.

3

•   G7   F   C   G7   Dm   Am   G7
Fa-ther, who did fash-ion me Im-age of your-self to be,
Am   G7   Dm   F   Am   G7   Dm   C
Fill me with your love div-ine, Let my ev-'ry thought be thine.

4

•   G7   F   C   G7   Dm   Am   G7
God, the bless-ed Three-in-One, Dwell with-in my heart a-lone;
Am   G7   Dm   F   Am   G7   Dm   C
As you give your-self to me May I give my-self to thee.

120 HH Singer, pg 129

PRAISE GOD FROM WHOM ALL BLESSINGS FLOW

C 4/4
↓ _ ↓ ↑
4 r m i t
3 A C E G
open C

Text: from Psalm 150; vs 1 by Thomas Ken, 1695, altered; vs 2,3 by Stephen J. Wolf, 2009
Music: OLD HUNDREDTH, LM, Louis Bourgeois, first published in *Genevan Psalter,* 1551

①   **C**   **Am**   **F**   **E7**
Praise God, from whom all bless-ings flow;
     C   **Am**   **F**   **G7**
Praise God, all crea-tures here be-low;
     G6   **E7**   **Am**   **C**
Praise God a-bove, ye heav'n-ly host!
     Am   **F**   **G6**   **C**   ↓
Praise Fa-ther, Son, and Ho-ly Ghost.

②   •   **Am**   **F**   **E7**
For maj-es-ty and migh-ty deeds,
     C   **Am**   **F**   **G7**
With blast of horn and tam-bou-rine,
     G6   **E7**   **Am**   **C**
With harp and dance and flute and string,
     Am   **F**   **G6**   **C**   ↓
Let ev'-ry hu-man breath now sing.

③   •   **Am**   **F**   **E7**
Give praise to reach the migh-ty dome,
     C   **Am**   **F**   **G7**
Give praise with cym-bals, crash-ing sound,
     G6   **E7**   **Am**   **C**
Give praise with lyre and bless-ed skill,
     Am   **F**   **G6**   **C**   ↓
Praise God to wake the ho-ly hill.

④   •   **Am**   **F**   **E7**
Praise God, from whom all bless-ings flow;
     C   **Am**   **F**   **G7**
Raise hands, all crea-tures here be-low;
     G6   **E7**   **Am**   **C**
Praise God, our Fa-ther and the Son
     Am   **F**   **G6**   **C**   ↓
And Ho-ly Spir-it, Three in One.

HH Singer, pg 52

PRAISE MY SOUL THE KING OF HEAVEN

$\frac{2}{4}$

↓ ↑ _ ↑
4 r m i t
3 A G E C
open G

Text: from Psalm 103, Henry F. Lyte, 1834, altered
Music: 87 87 87 LAUDA ANIMA, John Goss, 1869

①
    G7   •   C   Am
Praise, my soul, the King of heav-en;
  F   Am   F   Dm
To these feet your trib-ute bring.
  E7   •   Am   G7
Ran-somed, healed, re-stored, for-giv-en,
  G6 E7   C   G7
Ev-er-more God's prais-es sing:
  C Am C Am   •   F G7   C   ↓
Al-le-lu-ia! Al-le-lu-ia! Praise the ev-er-last-ing King.

②
    G7   •   C   Am
Praise for grace and fav-or giv-en
  F   Am   F   Dm
In our an-ces-tral dis-tress.
  E7   •   Am G7
Praise God, still the same as ev-er,
  G6 E7   C   G7
Slow to chide and swift to bless.
  C Am C Am   •   F   G7   C   ↓
Al-le-lu-ia! Al-le-lu-ia! Glo-rious love and faith-ful-ness.

③
    G7   •   C   Am
As a par-ent, tend-ing, spar-ing,
  F   Am   F   Dm
Well our fee-ble frame God knows.
  E7   •   Am G7
Gent-ly bear-ing and res-cu-ing
  G6 E7   C   G7
Us from all who'd be our foes.
  C Am C Am   •   F   G7   C   ↓
Al-le-lu-ia! Al-le-lu-ia! Wide-ly yet the mer-cy flows.

122 PRAISE THE LORD YOU HEAV'NS ADORE

HH Singer, pg 104

C 4/4
↓ ↑ _ ↑
4 r m i t
3 A G E C
open E

Text: St.1,2, Foundling Hospital Collection,1801; St.3, Edward Osler,1836,altered
Music: 87 87 D, PLEADING SAVIOR, Joshua Leavitt, *Christian Lyre*, 1830
Popular melody for: *Sing of Mary, Pure and Lowly*

1

```
    C           F           C         G6        C           F         G6          C
Praise the\ Lord, you/ heav'ns, a-dore\;  Praise you\ an-gels/ in the height;
  •         F           C         G6        C           F         G6          C
Sun and\ Moon, re/-joice be-fore\;  Shine your\ praise, you/ stars of light.
  G6        G7          F         Am        G6          G7          F          G7
Give praise\, for the Lord has\ spo-ken;  Might-y\ voice the worlds o\-beyed;
  C           F          C         Am        C           F          E7          C
Laws which\ nev-er/ shall be bro-ken,  Guid-ance\ that the/ Lord has made.
```

2

```
  •         F           C         G6        C        F          G6          C
Praise the\ Lord, the/ Lord is glo-rious,  Prom-is\-es that/ do not fail;
  •         F           C         G6        C        F          G6          C
God has\ made the/ saints vic-tor-ious,  Sin and\ death shall/ not pre-vail.
  G6        G7          F         Am        G6          G7          F          G7
Praise the\ God of our sal\-va-tion;  Hosts on\ high the pow'r pro\-claim;
  C           F          C         Am        C           F          E7          C
Heav-en and earth and/ all cre-a-tion,  Praise and\ mag-ni/-fy the name.
```

3

```
  •         F           C         G6        C           F         G6          C
Wor-ship\, hon-or/, glo-ry, bles-sing,  Lord, we\ off-er/ un-to thee;
  •         F           C         G6
Young and\ old, your/ praise ex-pres-sing,
  C         F           G6        C
In glad\ hom-age/ bend the knee.
  G6        G7          F         Am
All the\ saints in heav-en a-dore you,
  G6        G7          F         G7
We would\ bow be-fore your\ throne;
  C           F          C         Am        C           F          E7          C
As your\ an-gels/ serve be-fore you,  So on\ earth your/ will be done.
```

HH Singer, pg 128

PRAISE TO THE LORD THE ALMIGHTY

3/4
↓ ↑ ↓
4 tr m i
Claw A ↓ G

Text: from Nehemiah 9:6, Joachim Neander, 1679;
translated by Catherine Winkworth, 1863, altered; verse 2 by Stephen J. Wolf, 2009
Music: 14 14 4 7 8 LOBE DEN HERREN; Straslund Gesangbuch, 1665

open C

     C   E7   Am   F   Dm   G7 C ↓

① **Praise** to the Lord, the Al-migh-ty, the King of cre-a-tion!

  •   E7   Am   F   Dm   G7 C ↓

O my soul, praise the Lord, who is our health and sal-va-tion!

 G7   Am   C   G7   E7 ↓

Join the full throng; Wake, harp and psal-ter and song;

 G7   F   Dm C ↓

Sound forth in glad ad-o-ra-tion!

  •   E7   Am   F   Dm   G7 C ↓

② **Praise** to the Lord, the on-ly One, the Ma-ker of heav-en,

  •   E7   Am   F   Dm   G7 C ↓

It is the Lord who made the earth, the seas and all in them.

 G7   Am   C   G7   E7 ↓

Can we yet see How our de-sire\ and need

 G7   F   Dm C ↓

Meet in our Lord's will and un-ion.

  •   E7   Am   F   Dm   G7 C ↓

③ **Praise** to the Lord, who brings our work to pros-per be-fore us;

  •   E7   Am   F   Dm   G7 C ↓

Who from the heav-ens sent the mer-cy riv-er in-to us.

 G7   Am   C   G7   E7 ↓

Pon-der a-new What the Al-migh-ty can do,

 G7   F   Dm C ↓

Who in div-ine love be-friends us.

  •   E7   Am   F   Dm   G7 C ↓

④ **Praise** to the Lord, oh let all that is in us sing prais-ing!

  •   E7   Am   F   Dm   G7 C ↓

All that has life and breath, come forth and with us sing prais-ing!

 G7   Am   C   G7   E7 ↓

Let the A-men Sound from all peo-ple a-gain;

 G7   F   Dm C ↓

Glad-ly sing wor-ship and prais-ing!

124

HH Singer, pg 151

3/4
↑_ ↑↓ ↑_
4 *tr m i*
3 A E C A E G
open E

SHEPHERD OF SOULS

Text: James Mongtomery, 1825, altered
Music: ST. AGNES, CM, John B. Dykes, 1866

1

| C | G7 | F | C | G7 | C | G7 |

Shep-herd of souls, re-fresh and bless Your cho-sen pil-grim flock

| Dm | G7 | E7 | C | G7 | Am | C | Am |

With man-na in the wil-der-ness, And wa-ter from the rock.

2

| C | G7 | F | C | G7 | C | G7 |

Hung-ry and thirs-ty, mor-tal, weak, As you would come and go:

| Dm | G7 | E7 | C | G7 | Am | C Am |

Our souls the joys of heav-en seek Which from your pass-ion flow.

3

| C | G7 | F | C | G7 | C | G7 |

We would not live by bread a-lone, But by your Word of grace,

| Dm | G7 | E7 | C | G7 | Am | C | Am |

In strength of which we trav-el on To our a-bi-ding place.

4

| C | G7 | F | C | G7 | C | G7 |

Be known to us in break-ing bread, But do not then de-part;

| Dm | G7 | E7 | C | G7 | Am | C |

Sa-vior, a-bide with us and spread Your ta-ble in our heart.

HH Singer, pg 118

3/4
↓ ↑ ↓
4 *tr m i*
3 A E C A E G
Claw A ↓ G

open E

WE WALK BY FAITH

Text: CM, based on 2 Cor. 5:7 and John 20:24-29; Henry Alford, 1844, altered
Music: ST. AGNES, CM, John B. Dykes, 1866
Popular melody for: *Shepherd of Souls*, page 124
SHANTI, by Marty Haugen, GIA Publications, 1984, is a different current familiar tune.

① C G7 F C
We walk by faith, and not by sight;
G7 C G7
No gra-cious words we hear
Dm G7 E7 C
From him who spoke as none e'er spoke;
G7 Am C Am
But we be-lieve him near.

② C G7 F C
We may not touch his hands and side,
G7 C G7
Nor fol-low where he trod;
Dm G7 E7 C
But in his prom-ise we re-joice,
G7 Am C Am
And cry, "My Lord and God!"

③ C G7 F C
Help then, O Lord, our un-be-lief;
G7 C G7
And may our faith a-bound,
Dm G7 E7 C
To call on you when you are near
G7 Am C Am
And seek where you are found.

④ C G7 F C G7 C G7
That, when our life of faith is done, In realms of clear-er light
Dm G7 E7 C G7 Am C
We may be-hold you as you are, With full and end-less sight.

126

HH Singer, pg 145

THE CHURCH's ONE FOUNDATION

C 4/4
↓↑↓↑ 4 tr m i m
3 A C E G A C E G

Text: see Ephesians 2:20; Samuel J. Stone, 1866, altered
Music: 76 76 D, AURELIA, Samuel S. Wesley, 1864

open E

```
         C                    Am          Dm                  C
① The Church's one foun-da-tion   Is Je-sus Christ, her Lord;
       G7              Am         F                G7
   She is his new cre-a-tion   By wa-ter and the Word.
       G6              Am         C                F
   From heav'n he came and sought her   To be his ho-ly bride;
       E7              G7         F                C
   By blood re-deem-ing bought her,  And for her life he died.

  •                   Am          Dm                  C
② E-lect from ev-'ry na-tion,   Yet one o'er all the earth,
       G7              Am         F                G7
   Her char-ter of sal-va-tion   One Lord, one faith, one birth.
       G6              Am         C                F
   One ho-ly name she bless-es,  Par-takes one ho-ly food,
       E7              G7         F                C
   And to one hope she press-es,  With ev-'ry grace en-dued.

  •                   Am          Dm                  C
③ Though with a scorn-ful won-der  Some see her sore op-pressed,
       G7              Am         F                G7
   By schis-ms rent a-sun-der,   By her-e-sies dis-tressed,
       G6              Am         C                F
   Yet saints their watch are keep-ing;  Their cry goes up, "How long?"
       E7              G7         F                C
   And soon the night of weep-ing   Shall be the morn of song.

  •                   Am          Dm                  C
④ Mid toil and trib-u-la-tion   And tu-mult of her war
       G7              Am         F                G7
   She waits the con-sum-ma-tion   Of peace for-ev-er-more,
       G6              Am         C                F
   Til with the vis-ion glo-rious   Her long-ing eyes are blest
       E7              G7         F                C
   And the great Church vic-tor-ious   Shall be the Church at rest.
```

HH Singer, pg 116

OUR FATHER ALL CREATING

C 4/4
↓↑↓↑
4 tr m i m tr m i m
3 A C E G A C E G
open E

Text: John Ellerton, 1826-1893, altered significantly
Music: 76 76 D, AURELIA, Samuel S. Wesley, 1864
Popular melody for: *The Church's One Foundation*, page 126

①

  C   Am   Dm   C
Our Fa-ther, all cre-a-ting, Whose wis-dom, love, and pow'r
  G7   Am   F   G7
First bound two lives to-geth-er In E-den's pri-mal hour,
  G6   Am   C   F
To all this day in marr-iage Those ear-ly gifts re-new:
  E7   G7   F   C
In homes by you made hap-py In love by you kept true.

②

  •   Am   Dm   C
Lord, as with wine at Ca-na, The wed-ding feast you blessed,
  G7   Am   F   G7
Let spouses know the pres-ence Of you, their dear-est guest.
  G6   Am   C   F
Their store of earth-ly glad-ness Trans-form to heav'n-ly wine,
  E7   G7   F   C
And teach them in their trust-ing To know the gift div-ine.

③

  •   Am   Dm   C
O Spir-it of the Fa-ther And Son, give them your breath,
  G7   Am   F   G7
And strength of heart in pa-tience, Your ten-der love their wealth,
  G6   Am   C   F
That, guard-ed by your pres-ence And kept from strife with-in,
  E7   G7
Their hearts may sense your guid-ance
  F   C
And know you dwell with them.

128

C 4/4
↓ ↑ ↓ ↑
4 *tr m i m*
3 A C E G A C E G
Claw A E ↓ G
open E

WE PLOW THE FIELDS AND SCATTER

HH Singer, pg 148

Text: Matthias Claudius, 1782, hearing the words sung by farmers;
translated by Jane M. Campbell, 1861, altered
Music: 76 76 D, AURELIA, Samuel S. Wesley, 1864
Popular melody for: *The Church's One Foundation*, page 126

1

```
      C                    Am            Dm                      C
We plow the fields and scat-ter   the good seed on the land,
      G7                   Am            F                       G7
But it is fed and wa-tered   by God's al-migh-ty hand;
      G6                   Am            C                       F
God sends the snow in win-ter,   the warmth to swell the grain,
      E7                   G7            F                       C
The breezes and the sun-shine,   and soft refresh-ing rain.
```

2

```
       •              Am            Dm                      C
God on-ly is the Ma-ker   of all things near and far;
       G7                   Am            F                       G7
the Paint-er of the flow-er,   the Ligh-ter of the star;
       G6                   Am            C                       F
The winds and waves o-bey-ing,   while all the birds are fed;
       E7                   G7            F                       C
Much more as God's own chil-dren   are giv-en dai-ly bread.
```

3

```
       •              Am            Dm                      C
We thank you, then, O Fa-ther,   for all things bright and good,
       G7                   Am            F                       G7
The seed time and the har-vest,   our life, our health, our food;
       G6                   Am            C                       F
No gifts have we to off-er,   for all your love im-parts,
       E7                   G7            F                       C
But that which you de-sire\,   our hum-ble, thank-ful hearts.
```

HH Singer, pg 131

SINGULAR JUSTICE

6/4
↓ ↑ ↓
4 tr m i   or   rmit i t
3 A E C A E G   or   Claw A↓G
open C

Text: from Psalm 71, New American Bible, by Stephen J. Wolf, 2003,
tribute to the priesthood of Philip Breen
Music: 7777, THE CALL, Ralph Vaughan Williams, 1872-1958
Popular melody for: *Come My Way My Truth My Life*

SLOWLY

**① **

C	Em	Am	G7			

Of your sing-u-lar jus-tice we sing,

C   Em   Am   G7   C7   Am   C   G7
God, our trust, our hope\ from youth. In your jus-tice res-cue us.

F   Am   G6↓↑   F↓↑   G7↓↑   E7   C   •
Fill our lungs   with cause to sing your prais-es dai-ly.

**② **

•   Em   Am   G7
Do not cast a-side in old age

C   Em   Am   G7   C7   Am   C   G7
those of fail-ing strength\ or mind. Be our ref-uge strong, sec-ure,

F   Am   G6↓↑   F↓↑   G7↓↑   E7   C   •
shame us not   and show fi-del-i-ty   for all eyes.

**③ **

•   Em   Am   G7
God, you teach us from days\ of youth.

C   Em   Am   G7   C7   Am   C   G7
We pro-claim, 'til old\ and gray. Won-der, mer-cy, jus-tice, might,

F   Am   G6↓↑   F↓↑   G7↓↑   E7   C   •
to new gen -er -a- tions yet to know your stor-y.

**④ **

•   Em   Am   G7
We de-pend on you from our birth.

C   Em   Am   G7   C7   Am   C   G7
From af-flict-ion, wat-er-y deep, raise us up, re-vive, re-store,

F   Am   G6↓↑   F↓↑   G7↓↑   E7   C   •
help our harp and voice sing jus-tice, joy and won-der.

130 HH Singer, pg 19

TAKE LORD RECEIVE

C 3/4
↓ ↑ ↓
4 mr i t mr i t
3 A E C A E G
Claw A ↓ G
open C

Text: Verse 1: *The Serenity Prayer*, attributed to Reinhold Niebuhr, d. 1971
Verses 2-5: Suscipe from *The Spiritual Exercises* of St. Ignatius of Loyola, #234, d.1556,
inspired by *Veneremur*, Jesuit Spirituality Center, Grand Coteau, LA, 1957
Music: TALLIS CANON, LM, Thomas Tallis, d. 1585

1
```
     C          Am    G7  Am        F        C      G7        C
O God, grant me ser-en-i-ty   to'ac-cept the things I can-not change,
        F          C       G7       C
The cour-age to change the things I can,
        F         C       G7       C   • • •
and wis-dom to know the diff-er-ence.
```

2
```
 •          Am    G7   Am       F       C     G7       C
Take, Lord, re-ceive my lib-er-ty,  My will en-tire and mem-o-ry,
       F        C        G7       C     F        C     G7    C  • • •
My un-der-stand-ing, ev-'ry-thing, Pos-ses-sions all, my off-er-ing.
```

3
```
 •          Am    G7   Am         F       C    G7      C
The giv'n by you I do re-turn; Con-form my life as is your will.
       F        C       G7      C      F       C    G7    C  • • •
Suf-fic-ient now, no more to own: E-nough are love and grace a-lone.
```

4
```
 •     Am      G7      Am      F       C       G7          C
Lord A-do-nai, your love and grace, Suf-fic-ient these in time and space,
       F        C       G7        C
Your love and grace, un-earned and free,
       F        C       G7       C   • • •
This true a-bun-dance may we see.
```

5
```
 •          Am      G7       Am
Love show-ing more in deed than word,
       F       C      G7        C
Love sha-ring in the com-mon good,
       F       C       G7      C       F      C      G7       C • • •
I pon-der with a-ffec-tion great What God has done and does of late.
```

HH Singer, pg 125

BLEST HOLY

Text: based on Matthew 5:1-12a; Stephen J. Wolf, 2017
Music: JESU DULCIS MEMORIA, LM; Model 1
Popular melody for: *O Radiant Light, O Sun Divine*

↓ ↑ ↓
4 *tr m i*
3 A E C A E G
open E

        C   Am   F   Am   C   G   Em   C

① **Blest Ho-ly**, you in spir-it poor   held down in heav-y pov-er-ty;
   Am   F   C   D   Am   G7   E7   C   Am
   in full de-pend-ence on the Lord\\   yours is the roy-al realm of God.

        C   Am   F   Am   C   G   Em   C

② **Blest Ho-ly** too are you who mourn   shed-ing the tears of hu-man grief;
   Am   F   C   D   Am   G7   E7   C   Am
   they hon-or loss a-mid the pain\\;   re-mem-ber love, you'll laugh a-gain.

        C   Am   F   Am   C   G   Em   C

③ **Blest Ho-ly**, you who join the meek   em-brac-ing risk to fol-low Christ,
   Am   F   C   D   Am   G7   E7   C   Am
   mind, bo-dy, soul, and will-ing strength\\, in-her-it ho-ly land at length.

        C   Am   F   Am   C   G   Em   C

④ **Blest Ho-ly** hung-ry, you who thirst: with thirst and hung-er sat-is-fied
   Am   F   C   D   Am   G7   E7   C   Am
   in right-eous fair-ness, jus-tice due\\,   gen-u-ine joy in grat-i-tude.

        C   Am   F   Am   C   G   Em   C

⑤ **Blest Ho-ly**, you who mer-cy show,   re-ceived in mea-sure giv-en well:
   Am   F   C   D   Am   G7   E7   C   Am
   the great-est gift of Je-sus Christ\\,   so wise are all who claim this prize.

        C   Am   F   Am   C   G   Em   C

⑥ **Blest Ho-ly**, you the clean of heart,   in sing-le fo-cus on the good
   Am   F   C   D   Am   G7   E7   C   Am
   who live in free-dom blem-ish free\\, your cen-ter, God, whom you shall see.

        C   Am   F   Am   C   G   Em   C

⑦ **Blest Ho-ly**, you who seek for peace   be-yond what hu-mans un-der-stand,
   Am   F   C   D   Am   G7   E7   C   Am
   In pa-tient prayer and hon-est lis-ten-ing, as sons and daught-ers of the King.

        C   Am   F   Am   C   G   Em   C

⑧ **Re-joice** in glad-ness, last-ing joy,   who for the sake of what is right
   Am   F   C   D   Am   G7   E7   C   •
   bear per-se-cu-tion for the good\\\;   dwell safe-ly in the realm of God.

132   HH Singer, pg 141

¾   **WE GATHER TOGETHER**
↓_ ↓↑ ↓↑   Text: Dutch:*Wilt heden nu treden,* 1597, translated by Theodore Baker, 1894, altered
4 *tr i m*   Music: 12 11 12 11 KREMSER; *Nederlandtsche Gedenckclanck,* by Adrianus Valerius, 1626;
   or *t i mr*   arranged and translated from Dutch to Latin by Edward Kremser, 1877
3 A E C A E G

open G

1

```
         C          Am            F                    C
    We gath-er to-geth-er   to ask the Lord's bless-ing;
         G7              F             Dm              G7
    Who chast-ens and hast-ens  the Way to make known.
         C              F             G7              C
    The wick-ed op-press-ing   now cease/ from dis-tress-ing.
         F              C             G7              C
    Sing prais-es to the Name\;  God'for -gets not God's own.
```

2

```
  •      Am            F                    C
    Be-side us to guide us,   our God with us join-ing,
         G7              F             Dm              G7
    Or-dain-ing, main-tain-ing  the king-dom div-ine;
         C              F             G7              C
    So from the be-gin-ning   the fight/ we were win-ning,
         F              C             G7              C
    You, Lord, were at our side\,  all glo-ry be thine!
```

3

```
  •      Am            F                    C
    We all do ex-tol you,   our Lead-er tri-umph-ant,
         G7              F             Dm              G7
    And pray that you still   our De-fend-er will be.
         C              F             G7              C
    Let your con-gre-ga-tion   es-cape the trib-u-la-tion;
         F              C             G7              C
    Your Name be ev-er praised\!  O Lord, keep us free!
```

HH Singer, pg 105

WHAT A FRIEND WE HAVE IN JESUS

Text: based on Matthew 21:22; Joseph Scriven, 1865;
verse 2 Stephen J. Wolf, 2010
Music: FRIEND; Charles C. Converse, 1868

↓ _ ↓ ↑
4 tr m i m
3 A G E C A G E C
open G

1

```
       C       F            C  Am
What a Friend we have in Je-sus,
       C       Am           G7    E7
All our sins and griefs to bear!
       C       F            C  Am
What a priv-i-lege to car-ry
    C       G7           C       E7
Ev-'ry-thing to God in prayer!
    C       Am           F   G7
Oh, what peace we of-ten for-feit,
    C       Am           G7    E7
Oh, what need-less pain we bear,
    C       F            C   F
All be-cause we do not car-ry
    C       G7           C       E7
Ev-'ry-thing to God in prayer!
```

2

```
      C    F          C  Am   C   Am        G7   E7
Glo-ry be to God the Fa-ther, Son, and Spir-it ev-'ry-where.
      C    F          C  Am   C    G7           C    E7
Glo-ry be as the Be-got-ten  Son of Ab-ba hears our prayer
    C       Am                F   G7
At the right hand of the Fa-ther,
    C       Am           G7    E7
Lamb of God, our mer-cy home.
    C       F            C  F  C    G7           C    •
Fa-ther, Son and Ho-ly Spir-it, Glo-ry be to you a-lone.
```

134 HH Singer, pg 146

C 4/4
↓ ↑ ↓ ↑
4 r m i t
3 A C E G A C E G

2nd fret C

WHAT WONDROUS LOVE IS THIS

Text: attributed to Alexander Means, first appeared in 1811
Music: 12 9 12 12 9, WONDROUS LOVE; adapted by William Walker,
The Southern Harmony and Musical Companion, 1835

(1)
       G7   **F**   **G7**   **E7**
What won-drous love is this, O my soul, O my soul!
     C   **F**   **G7** ↓
What won-drous love is this, O my soul!
     F   **G7**   **C**   **G7**
What won-drous love is this that caused the Lord\ of bliss
E7   **F**   **G7**   **C**
To bear the dread-ful curse for my soul, for my soul,
Am   **F**   **G7** ↓
To bear the dread-ful curse for my soul.

(2)
                         F   **G7**   **E7**
To God and to the Lamb, I will sing, I will sing;
   C   **F**   **G7** ↓
To God and to the Lamb, I will sing.
   F   **G7**   **C**   **G7**
To God and to the Lamb who is the great\ "I Am";
E7   **F**   **G7**   **C**
While mil-lions join the theme, I will sing, I will sing;
Am   **F**   **G7** ↓
While mil-lions join the theme, I will sing.

(3)
                        F   **G7**   **E7**
And when from death I'm free, I'll sing on, I'll sing on;
   C   **F**   **G7** ↓
And when from death I'm free, I'll sing on.
   F   **G7**   **C**   **G7**
And when from death I'm free, I'll sing and joy\-ful be;
E7   **F**   **G7**   **C**
And through e-ter-ni-ty, I'll sing on, I'll sing on;
Am   **F**   **G7**   **C**↓
And through e-ter-ni-ty, I'll sing on.

HH Singer, pg 135

BE STILL MY SOUL

$\frac{4}{4}$

↓ ↑ _ ↓
4 r m i t
3 A C E G

open E

Text: Katherina von Schlegel; in *Neue Sammlung Geistlicher Lieder*, 1752;
translated by Jane Borthwick, 1813-1897
Music: 10 10 10 10 10 10 FINLANDIA; Jean Sibleius, 1865-1957

①
     G7   F •   G7   C   G7 E7 •
Be still, my soul   the Lord is at your side /!
     G7   F •   G7   C   Am • •
Bear pa-tient-ly   the cross of grief or pain;
     G7   F •   C   G7   • F •
Leave to your God   to or-der and pro-vide /
     C   Am •   C   G7   E7 • •
In ev-'ry change,   who faith-ful will re-main.
     C   F •   C   G7   • F •
Be still, my soul   your best, your heav'n-ly friend /
     C   Am •   F   G7   C • •
Through thorn-y ways   leads to a joy-ful end.

②
     G7   F •   G7   C   G7 E7 •
Be still, my soul   your God does un-der-take /
     G7   F •   G7   C   Am • •
To guide the fu-   ture as God has the past;
     G7   F •   C   G7   • F •
Your hope, your con-   fi-dence let noth-ing shake /
     C   Am •   C   G7   E7 • •
All now mys-te-   rious shall be bright at last.
     C   F •   C   G7   • F •
Be still, my soul   the waves and winds still know /
     C   Am •   F   G7   C • •
His voice who ruled   while dwell-ing here be-low.

③
     G7   F •   G7   C   G7 E7 •
Be still, my soul   the hour is has-t'ning on /
     G7   F •   G7   C   Am • •
When we shall be   for-ev-er with the Lord,
     G7   F •   C   G7   • F •
When dis-ap-point-   ment, grief, and fear are gone /,
     C   Am •   C   G7   E7 • •
Sor-row for-got,   love's pur-est joys re-stored.
     C   F •   C   G7   • F •
Be still, my soul   when change and tears are past /,
     C   Am •   F   G7   C • •
All safe and bless-   ed we shall meet at last.

136

HH Singer, pg 72

C 4/4
↓ ↑ _ ↑
4 *r m i t*
3 A G E C
open E

HOLY MARY GRACEFUL MOTHER

Text: Verses 1B & 2 by John Newton, *Olney Hymns*, 1779
Music: 87 87 D, PLEADING SAVIOR, Joshua Leavitt, *Christian Lyre*, 1830
Popular melody for: *Sing of Mary, Pure and Lowly*

1
    C   F   C   G6
Ho-ly\ Ma-ry/, grace-ful Mo-ther,
    C   F   G6   C
hear your\ sons and/ daugh-ters say,
   •   F   C   G6
Mo-ther\, Bless-ed/ a-mong wo-men,
    C   F   G6   C
for your\ sons and/ daugh-ters, pray.
   G6   G7   F   Am
May the\ grace of Christ our\ Sa-vior
   G6   G7   F   G7
And the\ Fa-ther's bound-less\ love
    C   F   C   Am
With the\ Ho-ly/ Spir-it's fa-vor
    C   F   E7   C
Rest up\-on us/ from a-bove.

2
   •   F   C   G6
Thus may\ we a/-bide in u-nion
    C   F   G6   C
With each\ oth-er/ and the Lord,
   •   F   C   G6
And pos\-sess, in/ sweet com-mu-nion,
    C   F   G6   C
Joys which\ earth can/-not af-ford.
   G6   G7   F   Am
May the\ grace of Christ our\ Sa-vior
   G6   G7   F   G7
And the\ Fa-ther's bound-less\ love
    C   F   C   Am
With the\ Ho-ly/ Spir-it's fa-vor
    C   F   E7   C
Rest up\-on us/ from a-bove.

HH Singer, pg 106   137

HOLY JOSEPH

C 4/4
↓ ↑ _ ↑
4 *r m i t*
3 A G E C

Text: anonymous, altered significantly
Music: 87 87 D, PLEADING SAVIOR, Joshua Leavitt, *Christian Lyre*, 1830
Popular melody for: *Sing of Mary, Pure and Lowly*

open E

❶

```
  C        F        C   G6      C        F        G6       C
Ho-ly\ Jo-seph/, you sa-lut-ing Here we\ meet, with/ hearts sin-cere;
  •        F        C   G6      C        F        G6       C
Bless-ed\ Jos-eph/, all u-nite and  Call on\ you to/ hear our prayer.
  G6       G7       F    Am      G6       G7       F        G7
Hap-py\ saint in hea-ven a-dor-ing  Je-sus\, Sa-vior of the\ race,
            C        F        C        Am
          Hear your\ fost-er/ sons and daugh-ters,
            C        F        E7       C
          May we\ find with/ you our place.
```

❷

```
  C        F        C   G6      C        F        G6       C
You who\ faith-ful/-ly at-tend-ed Him whom\ heav'n and/ earth a-dore;
  •        F        C   G6      C        F        G6       C
Who with\ ten-der/ care de-fend-ed  Mar-y\, Vir-gin/ ev-er pure.
  G6       G7       F    Am      G6       G7       F        G7
May our\ trust-ing voic-es\ lift-ing  Move you\ for our souls to\ pray;
  C        F        C    Am      C        F        E7       C
May your\ smile of/ peace des-cend-ing,  Be-ne\-dic-tions/ on us lay.
```

❸

```
           C        F        C   G6      C        F        G6       C
Through this\ life, give/ watch a-round us!  Thank our\ Lord for/ ev-'ry breath,
             •        F        C        G6
           And, when\ part-ing/ fear sur-rounds us,
             C        F        G6       C
           Guide us\ e-ven/ through our death.
  G6       G7       F    Am      G6       G7       F        G7
Hap-py\ saint in hea-ven a-dor-ing  Je-sus\, Sa-vior of the\ race,
            C        F        C        Am
          Hear your\ fost-er/ sons and daugh-ters,
            C        F        E7       C
          May we\ find with/ you our place.
```

138

HH Singer, pg 41

C
↓ ↑ ↓
4 *tr i m*
3 A E C A E G
open G

O SANCTISSIMA

Text: *Stimmen der Volker in Liedern,* 1807
Music: 55 7 55 7, O DU FROLICHE; Tattersall's *Improved Psalmody,* 1704

```
 C   F  G7   Am  F    ↓
O sanc-tis-si-ma /,
 C   F  G7   Am  F    ↓
O pi-is-si-ma /,
 C   •   F  G7   E7 Am C   ↓
Dul-cis vir-go Ma-ri \- a!
 G6  G7      F  Dm
Ma/-ter a-ma/-ta,
 E7    G7      C  G7
In/ te-me-ra/-ta,
 F Am   F  C   E7 G7  C    ↓
O\-ra\, O\-ra\ pro-no\-bis.
```

2

```
  •  F  G7   Am  F    ↓
Ho-ly, ho-ly Ma-ry,
    C    F  G7     Am  F   ↓
Strong and hum-ble Ma-ry,
   C   •    F  G7    E7 Am C   ↓
Sweet-ness, vir-gin Ma-ri \- a!
 G6     G7      F  Dm
Moth-er of our Sa/-vior,
 E7     G7     C      G7
In your fi-at "yes" all for,
 F Am   F  C   E7 G7      C    ↓
O\-ra\, O\-ra\, pray \ for us.
```

HH Singer, pg 140

ON THIS DAY O BEAUTIFUL MOTHER

Text: Louis Lambillotte, SJ, 1796-1855, altered
Music: 77 77, BEAUTIFUL MOTHER, Rohr's *Favorite Catholic Melodies,* 1857

↓ ↑ ↓
4 *tr m i*
3 A E C A E G
open E

REFRAIN
```
      C        G7       F       Dm  C    ↓
On\ this day, O beau-ti-ful Mo-ther,
      Am       G7       Dm          Am   ↓
On\ this day we give you our love.
      C        G7       F       Dm  C    ↓
Near you, Ma-don-na, fond-ly we hov-er,
      Am       G7       Dm          C
Trust-ing your gen-tle care/ to prove.
```

```
         •       F       Am       C
① On this day we ask to share,
         •       F       Dm       C
   Dear-est Mo-ther, your sweet care;
        G7       F       C       F      G7↓
   Help us 'lest our feet\ a-stray\,
         •       F       C       G7     ↓
   Wand-'ring from your guid-ing way.         REFRAIN
```

```
         •       F       Am       C
② Queen of an-gels, deign to hear
         •       F       Dm       C
   Lisp-ing chil-dren's hum-ble pray'r;
        G7       F       C       F      G7↓
   Young hearts gain, O Vir\-gin pure\
         •       F       C       G7     ↓
   Sweet-ly to your-self al-lure.              REFRAIN
```

140   HH Singer, pg 28

STEPHEN DEACON PROTO-MARTYR

C 4/4
↓ ↑ ↓ ↑
4 r m i t
3 A G E C
open A (low)

Text: *Saint of God, Elect and Precious,* 11th C.; translated from Latin by John M. Neale, 1852;
adapted by Stephen J. Wolf for the dedication of *St. Stephen Church* on February 2, 2008
Music: 87 87 87 PICARDY, *Chansons Populaires des Provinces de France,* 1860,
Popular melody for: *Let All Mortal Flesh Keep Silence,* page 91

(1)
```
     F       C     Am  •  G6  •   Am      F    Dm Am    C      •
   Ste-phen, dea-con, pro-to\-mar-tyr, Gift-ed with the Spir-it of God,
     F       C     Am  •  G6  •   Am      F    Dm Am    C      •
   Wis-dom, faith and grace, work-ing won-ders, Speak-ing with an-gel-ic\ word,
     Am      F    G7 • Am    ↓↑    C  G7 •  C       F     G7  E7  Am  •
   Who when dy-ing did com-mend/ to\ God Your at-tack-ers with your/ soul.
```

(2)
```
     F       C     Am  •  G6  •   Am      F    Dm Am    C      •
   Tell/, Ste-phen, tell God's\ sto-ry: Cov-e-nent-ed A-bra\-ham,
     F       C     Am  •  G6  •   Am      F    Dm Am    C      •
   Jo-seph res-cued from his af-flic-tion, Mo-ses raised in Phar-oah's\ land,
     Am      F    G7 • Am    ↓↑    C     G7                  •
   At the burn-ing bush, stand-ing on ho-ly ground,
      C      F    G7  E7  Am           •
   Sent to set God's peo-ple/ free.
```

(3)
```
     F       C     Am  •  G6  •
   Wear-ing now the crown of a mar-tyr,
     Am      F    Dm Am    C      •
   In your lang-uage "Crown" your\ name.
     F       C     Am  •  G6  •
   You we ask to pray to the Fa-ther
     Am      F    Dm Am         C      •
   That when we are faced with the same,
     Am      F    G7 • Am    ↓↑    C          G7            •
   We may faith-ful be  free\ from fear and shame
      C      F    G7  E7  Am           •
   Show-ing mer-cy in God's/ name.
```

(4)
```
     F       C     Am  •  G6  •   Am      F    Dm Am    C      •
   Praise to God and thanks be to Je-sus, Who has shown us how to for-give,
     F       C     Am  •  G6  •   Am      F    Dm Am    C      •
   Pres-ent with the Ho-ly\ Spir-it They your vis-ion seen as you fell.
     Am      F    G7 • Am    ↓↑    C     G7                  •
   Called to serve the poor, then giv-en voice to preach,
      C      F    G7  E7  Am           •
   Pray we look to heav-en as well.
```

HH Singer, pg 94   141

C ⁴⁄₄   **FOR ALL THE SAINTS**
↓ _ ↓ ↑   Text: William H. How, 1864, altered
4 *r m i t*   Music: 10 10 10 SINE NOMINE with alleluias, by Ralph Vaughan Williams, 1906
3 A G E C A G E C
open G

                C   **F**   **C**

① **For all** the saints who from their la-bors rest,
    G7   **E7**   **F**   **G7**
   Who you by faith be-fore the world con-fess
  C   **G7**   **Dm**   **G7**   **F**   **C** **G7**   **C**
Your name, O Je-sus, be for-ev\-er\ blest, A /-le\-lu-ia! A/ /- le-lu-ia!

                C   **F**   **C**

② **You were** their rock, their for-tress and their might;
    G7   **E7**   **F**   **G7**
   You, Lord, their cap-tain in the well-fought fight;
  C   **G7**   **Dm**   **G7**   **F**   **C** **G7**   **C**
You, in the dark of night, their one\ true\ light. A /-le\-lu-ia! A/ /-le-lu-ia!

                C   **F**   **C**

③ **O blest** com-mu-nion, ho-ly and div-ine,
    G7   **E7**   **F**   **G7**
   While yet we strug-gle, they in glo-ry shine;
  C   **G7**   **Dm**   **G7**   **F**   **C** **G7**   **C**
Yet all are one in you, for all\ are\ thine. A /-le\-lu-ia! A/ /-le-lu-ia!

                C   **F**   **C**

④ **So when** there breaks a yet more glo-rious day,
    G7   **E7**   **F**   **G7**
   The saints tri-umph-ant rise in bright ar-ray;
  C   **G7**   **Dm**   **G7**   **F**   **C** **G7**   **C**
The King of Glo-ry pass-es on\ the\ Way. A /-le\-lu-ia! A/ /-le-lu-ia!

                C   **F**   **C**

⑤ **From earth's** wide bounds, from o-cean's farth-est coast,
    G7   **E7**   **F**   **G7**
   Through gates of pearl stream in the count-less host,
  C   **G7**   **Dm**   **G7**   **F**   **C** **G7**   **C**
Sing to the Fa-ther, Son, and Ho\-ly\ Ghost: A /-le\-lu-ia! A/ /-le-lu-ia!

142

HH Singer, pg 30

LORD GOD SABAOTH EL ADONAI

6/8
↓_ ↓↑ ↓_
4 tr m i
3 A E C A E G
open A (low)

Text: Ezekiel 36:24-28, Stephen J. Wolf, *Anger the Jesus Way*, 2016
Music: 888, O FILII ET FILIAE; Chant Mode II, *Airs sur les hymnes sacrez, odes et noels*, 1623
Popular melody for: *Ye Sons And Daughters*, page 73

①
    F   C   G7   F
Lord God /, Sab-a-oth, El, A-do-nai,
 •   C   G7   F
Proph-et E-ze-ki-el's song we lift high:
 •   Am   C   E7   G7   Am
Spir-it and heart \, re-newed you pro-↘vide,   You are our God…

REFRAIN
    Am   F   C   E7 G7   Am   ↓
You are our God \, your peo-ple are we, A – le – lu - ia!

---

②
    F   C   G7   F
Take us out-side of our pride that div-ides,
 •   C   G7   F
Gath-er us in from all na\-tions wide,
 •   Am   C   E7   G7   Am
Bring us back in-to your land at your ↘side,   You are our God…   **REFRAIN**

③
    F   C   G7   F
Sprin-kle on-to us your wa\-ters clean,
 •   C   G7   F
From our im-pur-i-ties help us to wean,
 •   Am   C   E7   G7   Am
Clean from i-dol-a-try let us be ↘seen,   You are our God…   **REFRAIN**

④
    F   C   G7   F
Take from our flesh\ these hearts\ of stone,
 •   C   G7   F
Make in us new hearts of flesh, not of bone,
 •   Am   C   E7   G7   Am
In-side our be-ing your Spir-it be ↘shown,   You are our God…   **REFRAIN**

⑤
    F   C   G7   F
Praise to you Fa-ther, and praise to you Son,
 •   C   G7   F
Praise to you Spir-it, three prais-es in One.
 •   Am   C   E7   G7   Am
Just-ice and Mer-cy un-til days are ↘done.   You are our God…   **REFRAIN**

HH Singer, pg 87 143

C 4/4
↓ ↑ ↓ ↑
4 *r m i t*
3 A G E C
open G (low)

LET US BREAK BREAD TOGETHER

Text: Spiritual
Music: 10 10 with refrain LET US BREAK BREAD, Spiritual

①   **C**   **G7**   **C**   **Am**
Let us break bread to-geth-er on our knees;
     G7   **F**   **G7**   **C**
Let us break bread to-geth-er on our knees;
    G7   •   **F**   **Dm**
When I fall on my knees, With my face to the ris-ing sun,
 Am   **F**   **C** ↓
O/ Lord, have mer-cy on_ me.

②   •   **G7**   **C** **Am**
Let us drink wine to-geth-er on our knees;
     G7   **F**   **G7** **C**
Let us drink wine to-geth-er on our knees;
    G7   •   **F**   **Dm**
When I fall on my knees, With my face to the ris-ing sun,
 Am   **F**   **C** ↓
O/ Lord, have mer-cy on_ me.

③   •   **G7**   **C** **Am**
Let us praise God to-geth-er on our knees;
     G7   **F**   **G7** **C**
Let us praise God to-geth-er on our knees;
    G7   •   **F**   **Dm**
When I fall on my knees, With my face to the ris-ing sun,
 Am   **F**   **C** ↓
O/ Lord, have mer-cy on_ me.

144   HH Singer, pg 144

3/4   **AMERICA (My Country 'tis of Thee)**

↓_↓↑↓_ or ↑_↑↓↑_   Text: Samuel F. Smith, d. 1895
4 tr m i   Music: 66 4 666 4 AMERICA; *Thesaurus Musicus*, 1744
3 A E C A E G
Claw A ↓ G
open C

    C   G7   E7   Am   G7   C
① **My coun-try, 'tis of thee,** Sweet land of lib-er-ty, Of thee I sing;
   G7   C   F   G7
   Land where my fa-thers died, Land of the pil-grims' pride,
   C   Am   F   C ↓
   From ev\-'ry\ moun-tain-side Let\ free-dom ring!

    C   G7   E7   Am
② **My** na-tive coun-try, thee, Land of the no-ble free,
   G7   C
   Thy name I love;
   G7   C   F   G7
   I love thy rocks and rills, Thy woods and tem-pled hills;
   C   Am   F   C ↓
   My heart\ with\ rap-ture thrills, Like\ that a-bove.

    C   G7   E7   Am
③ **Let** mu-sic swell the breeze, And ring from all the trees
   G7   C
   Sweet free-dom's song;
   G7   C   F   G7
   Let mor-tal tongues a-wake; Let all that breathe par-take;
   C   Am   F   C ↓
   Let rocks\ their\ si-lence break, The\ sound pro-long.

    C   G7   E7   Am   G7   C
④ **Our** fa-ther's God, to thee, Au-thor of lib-er-ty, To thee we sing;
   G7   C   F   G7
   Long may our land be bright With free-dom's ho-ly light;
   C   Am   F   C ↓
   Pro-tect\ us\ by thy might, Great\ God, our King.

145

THE LORD's PRAYER
Based on the Traditional Chant

↓ ↑ ↓ ↑
or ↓ (with thumb) holding the chords
4 *tr m i m*
3 G C E A
open E

    C   G7
Our Fa-ther
          F   C
who art in heav-en,
 G7   E7
hal-lowed be thy name.
  F   G7
Thy king-dom come,
  F   G7
thy will be done
    G6   G7 •   C
on earth as it is in heav-en.
  F   G7   E7   G7
Give_ us this day_ our dai-ly bread
     C   F   C •
and for-give us our tres-pass-es,
  •   C7   F   G7 •
as we for-give those who tres-pass a-gainst/ us,
  F   Am   G7 •
and lead us not in-to temp-ta/-tion,
  F   G7   C •
but de-liv-er us from e \-vil.

Am • C •
A - men.

CHORD PROGRESSIONS

MELODIES – *Song Titles*, page numbers
1st Note of the Song   CHORD PROGRESSION
("_" means the 1st Chord is NOT on 1st Beat)

Strumming Patterns
↓down ↑up
_ without hitting strings
← 4 finger Picking Patterns
← 3 finger Picking Patterns

4 finger picking:
A string   *r* (up↑ with the **ring** finger)
E string   *m* (up↑ with the **middle** finger)
C string   *i* (up↑ with the **index** finger)
G string   *t* (down↓ with the **thumb**)

3 finger Picking:
A string   A (up↑ always with the **middle** finger)
E string   E (up↑ always with the **index** finger)
C string   C (down↓ always with the **thumb**)
G string   G (down↓ always with the **thumb**)

Clawhammer:
A string **index** down
↓All Strings down
G string **thumb** down

ADESTE FIDELIS – *O Come All Ye Faithful*, 27
   open C   _C • G7 • E7 • C G7   F G7 F G7 E7 Am G7 •   C • Am C G7 C G7 •   ↓↑↓↑   4 *r m i t*
   REFRAIN   C G7 ↓↑ C •   E7 Am ↓↑ C G7   C G7 ↓↑ E7 C↓↑ F   C G7 C ↓   3 A C E G

ADORE TE DEVOTE 11 11 11 11 – *At The Name of Jesus*, 43 – *O My God My God Why*, 44   ↓↑
   open C   C G7 • • F G7 C ↓   C G7 • • F G7 C ↓   4 *tr m i*   3 A G E C
          G7 F C G7 F Dm E7 ↓   C F Dm • C G7 C ↓   Claw A ↓ G

AMERICA 66 4 666 4– *America (My Country 'tis of Thee)*, 144   ↓_↓↑↓_
   open C   C G7 E7 Am G7 C   G7 C F G7   C Am F C ↓   4 *tr m i*   3 A E C A E G

ANTIOCH, CM – *Joy To The World*, 26   ↓↑↓↑
   3rd fret A   C F C • G7 • C • F • G7 • C • • •   F • C • F • C •   *tr m i m*
          • • G7 • Dm • F •   C • • • G7 • C •   A C E G

AURELIA 76 76 D – *The Church's One Foundation*, 126 – *The Day Of Resurrection*, 70   ↓↑↓↑
       – *Our Father All Creating*, 127 – *We Plow The Fields And Scatter*, 128   *tr m i m*
   open E   _C Am Dm C   G7 Am F G7   G6 Am C F   E7 G7 F C   A C E G A C E G

BEAUTIFUL MOTHER 77 77 – *On This Day O Beautiful Mother*, 139   ↓↑↓
   open E   REFRAIN   C G7 F Dm C ↓   Am G7 Dm Am ↓   C G7 F Dm C ↓   Am G7 Dm C   *tr m i*
         VERSES   • F Am C   • F Dm C   G7 F C F G7↓   • F C G7 ↓   A E C A E G

BUNESSAN 5554 D (Morning Has Broken) – *As Abba Loves You*, 81   *r m t i*   ↓↑
   open C   C • Dm G7 F C   C6 Em Am G6 G7   C F Dm C Am D   G7 C F G7 C   A E C A E G

CAROL, CMD – *It Came Upon The Midnight Clear*, 25   ↓_↓↑↓_
   open G (low)   _C F C • F Am G7 •   C F C • F G7 C •   *tr i m*
          E7 • Am C   F Dm G7 •   C F C • F G7 C ↓   A E C A E G

CONDITOR, LM – *Creator Of The Stars Of Night*, 6   *tr i m*   ↓↑
   open E   _C G7 F G7   F C Am E7   F Am • C   Am G7 Am E7 G7   A E C A E G

DIADEMATA – *Crown Him With Many Crowns*, 46 (for Lent), 62 (for Easter), 89 (for Ordinary Time)   ↓_↓↑
   open C   C Am F • C F G7 •   C F D G7 Am F G7 •   *r m i t*
          C G7 F Am F G7 E7 G7   C F G7 C F G7 C •   A G E C

DIVINUM MYSTERIUM 87 87 87 7 – *Of The Father's Love Begotten*, 31   ↓↑↓↑
   open C   C Am C Am F↓   C G7 C ↓ G7 ↓   F Am C Am F↓   Am F G7 ↓ C↓   *r m i t*
          • Am C G7 C ↓ G7↓   C Am C G7↓   C Am C G7 C↓   A C E G

DIX 77 77 77 – *For The Beauty Of The Earth*, 94 – *Glady Magi From Of Old*, 19   ↓_↓↑
   open C   C G7 F C Am F G7 C   • G7 F C Am F G7 C   *tr m i m*
          • Am G7 C Am F G6 C •   A C E G

DUKE STREET, LM – *From All That Dwell Below The Skies*, 92 – *I Know That My Redeemer Lives*, 93   ↓_↓↑
   open C   C G7 C G7   • Am F G7   G6 C Am Dm   G7 Am G6 C   *r m i t*   A G E C

CHORD PROGRESSIONS

EASTER HYMN 77 77 with alleluias – *Jesus Christ Is Ris'n Today*, 68   ↓↑↓↑
    open C   C G7 F Am C F G6 C   F Am F G6 C F G6 C   *r m i t*
                G7 Dm C G6 G7 C E7 G7   • C F Am C Am G7 C   A C E G

EIN' FESTE BURG 87 87 66 66 7 – *A Mighty Fortress Is Our God*, 76   ↓↑↓↑
    open G   _ G D G D •   D7 • C G •   • D G D •   D7 • C G •   *r m i t*
               • C D • • C G •   • C D • C Am E7 •   D7 • C G •   A G E C

ELLACOMBE 76 76 D – *I Sing The Mighty Pow'r Of God*, 101   ↓↑↓↑
    open G (low)   _ C G7 C G7 Am G7 E7 ↓   C G7 C G7 Am F C ↓   *r m i t*
                  Am • G7 • Am • G7 ↓   C G7 C G7 Am F C ↓   A G E C

ENDLESS SONG 87 87 – *How Can I Keep From Singing*, 98   ↓↑_↑
    open G (low)   _ C E7 F Dm C G7 Am G7   C E7 F Dm C E7 F C   *r m i t*
                  G7 C F C Am F Am G7   C G7 Am G6 C Am G7 C   A C E G

ERHALT UNS HERR, LM – *The Glory Of These Forty Days*, 56 – *Take Up Your Cross*, 57   ↓↑_↑
           – *The God Whom Earth And Sea And Sky*, 36   *r m i t*
    open A (low)   _ C E7 C F   G7 Am G7 Am   F C G7 C   F C Dm Am •   A C E G

ES IST EIN' ROS' ENTSPRUNGEN 76 76 6 76 – *Lo, How a Rose E'er Blooming*, 41   ↓↑_↑
    open G   C G6 F C Am F Am↓↑ G7 Am G7↓↑ C ↓   • G6 F C Am   *r m i t*
        F Am↓↑ G7 Am G7↓↑ C ↓   G7 C G7 ↓   C F C Am F Am↓↑ G7 Am G7↓↑ C ↓   A C E G

FESTIVAL CANTICLE – *Great Are The Works of the Lord*, 95   ↓_↓↑
    3rd fret A   REFRAIN   _ Am F G7 F E7 C   • F G7 C C7 F G7 C↓   *r m i t*
                VERSES   G7 • F G7 C Am •   F Am C Am F G7 C ↓   A G E C

FINLANDIA 10 10 10 10 10 10 – *Be Still My Soul*, 135   ↓↑_↑
    open E   _ G7 F • G7 C G7 E7 •   G7 F • G7 C Am • •   G7 F • C G7 • F •   *r m i t*
              C Am • C G7 E7 • •   C F • C G7 • F •   C Am • F G7 C • •   A C E G

FOREST GREEN 86 86 86 86 – *O Lord Of Life*, 118
    open G (low)   _ C C7 Am G7   F G7 C •   • C7 Am G7   F G7 C •   ↓_↓↑
                  G7 C Am G7   C G7 E7 •   C F G7 C   F G7 C •   *r m i t*   A C E G

FRIEND – *What A Friend We Have In Jesus*, 133   ↓_↓↑
    open G   C F C Am   C Am G7 E7   C F C Am   C G7 C E7   *tr m i m*
              C Am F G7   C Am G7 E7   C F C F   C G7 C   E7   A G E C A G E C

GENEVA 42 87 87 77 88 – *Comfort Comfort O My People*, 5, 88   ↓↑↓ & ↓↑↓↑
    open C   C Am F↓↑↓↑ G7↓↑↓↑   C Am E7↓↑↓↑ C↓↑↓↑   *tr m i & r m i t*
              C Am F↓↑↓↑ G7↓↑↓↑   C Am E7↓↑↓↑ C↓↑↓↑   A G E C & A G E C
              Am G7 Am↓↑↓↑ G7↓↑↓↑   G7 Am F↓↑↓↑ E7↓↑↓↑
              C F C↓↑↓↑ Am↓↑↓↑   Am F G7↓↑↓↑ C↓↑↓↑ ↓↑↓↑

GLORIA 77 77 with refrain – *Angels We Have Heard On High*, 17   ↓↑↓↑
    open E   C Am G7 Am   C Am G6 C   • Am G7 Am   C Am G6 C   *r m i t*
          GLORIA   • Am F G7 C F G7 G6 C Am C G7   C Am F G7 C F G7 G6 C Am C G7 C •   A C E G

Go Tell It On The Mountain, 20   ↓↑↓↑
    open C   _ C • • •   G7 • C •   • • • •   Dm • G7 ↓   *tr m i m*
          REFRAIN   C • • •   G7 • C F   C • • •   Am G7 C ↓   A C E G

GOD REST YOU MERRY 86 86 86 with refrain – *God Rest Ye Merry Gentle Folk*, 21   ↓↑↓↑
    open A (low)   Am C F Am • F C •   Am C F Am • F C •   *tr m i m*
                   F C G7 C Am G7 E7   A C E G
          REFRAIN   F C F E7 • Am   C G7   F C G7 E7 • Am • ↓

148 CHORD PROGRESSIONS

GREENSLEEVES 87 87 with refrain – *What Child Is This*, 40 ↓↑↓
open A (low)   _Am • G7 • F • E7 •   Am • G7 • Am E7 Am •   tr m i
              C • G7 • Am • E7 •   C • G7 • Am E7 Am •   A G E C

GROSSER GOTT 78 78 77 – *Holy God We Praise Your Name*, 96 ↓↑↓
open C   C Am G7 C   Am F G7 Am G7↓   C Am G7 C   Am F G7 Am G7↓   tr m i
          G7 F C G7 F G7 F C   A E C A E G

HAMBURG – *When I Survey The Wondrous Cross*, 55 ↓↑_↑
open C   C E7 F C   • G7 F G7   C E7 F C   • F G7 C   r m i t r m i t   A C E G A C E G

HEINLEIN 7 7 7 7 – *Forty Days and Forty Nights*, 47 – *Come Redeemer Of Our Race*, 3 ↓_↓↑
open E   C F Am C   • G7 F E7   • F G7 C   • G7 E7 Am ↓   r m i t   A C E G

HYFRYDOL 87 87 D – *Alleluia! Sing To Jesus*, 60 – *Love Divine All Love Excelling*, 112 ↑_↑↓ ↑↓ or ↓_↓↓ ↓_
 – *Prophets Out of Ancient Times*, 113 – *There's A Wideness In God's Mercy*, 114   or ↓↑↓
open C   C Am F G7   C Am G7 C   • Am F G7   C Am G7 C   tr i m
          • Am F Dm   C Am Dm G7   C Dm C G7   C F G7 C   A E C A E G

HYMN TO JOY 8787D – *Joyful Joyful We Adore You*, 85 – *Blessed Be*, 84 – *Sing With All The Saints In Glory*, 69 ↓↑_↑
open E   C F G7 E7 C E7 Am G7   C F G7 E7 C Dm G7 C   tr m i m or r m i t
          G7 C G7 C G7 E7 Am G7   C F G7 E7 C Dm G7 C ↓   A G E C

IHR KINDERLEIN KOMMET 11 11 11 11 – *O Come Little Children*, 28   ↓_↓↑ r m i t r m i t
open G   _C • G7 C   • Am G7 C   G7 • C F   C Am G7 C •   A C E G A C E G

ITALIAN HYMN (MOSCOW) 664 6664 – *Lord Your Almighty Word (Let There Be Light)*, 110   ↓_↓↑↓_ tr m i tr m i
open G   C G7 C   • F G7   C G6   G7 Am G7 Am   C G7 F C↓   A E C A E G

JESU DULCIS MEMORIA, LM (*O Radiant Light O Sun Divine*) – *Lord Of All Being Throned Afar*, 108   tr m i ↓↑↓
 – *To You We Owe Our Hymn of Praise*, 109 – *Blest Holy (The Beatitudes)*, 131   tr i m
open E   C Am F Am   C G7 Em C   Am F C D   Am G7 E7 C   A E C A E G

KINGS OF ORIENT 88 44 6 with refrain – *We Three Kings Of Orient Are*, 39   ↓_↓↑↓_
open E   Am • E7 Am   • • E7 Am   C G7 Am F   Dm E7 Am •   tr m i
REFRAIN   G7 •   C • F C   • • F C   • G7 F G7   C • F C Am↓   A E C A E G

KINGSFOLD, CMD – *I Heard The Voice Of Jesus Say*, 100 – *Praise To The Holiest In The Height*, 52   ↓↑_↑
open C   _F Am C G7 C Dm G7 •   F Am C G7 C Dm Am •   tr m i m
         G7 C F Am C F G7 •   F Am C G7 C Dm Am ↓   A C E G

KREMSER 12 11 12 11 – *We Gather Together*, 132   ↓↑↓   tr i m or tr m i
open G   _C Am F C   G7 F Dm G7   C F G7 C   F C G7 C   A E C A E G

LAMBILLOTTE, LM – *Come Holy Spirit Whoever One*, 87   ↓↑↓   t i m r
open G (low)   C F G7 Am   • G7 Am G7   C F G7 Am   C F C G7   C F G7 C   A E C A E G

LAND OF REST 86 86 CM – *Jerusalem My Happy Home*, 103   ↓↑↓ tr m i
open G (low)   _C G7 F G7   C G7 Em •   F Am C G6   Am F C •   A E C A E G

LASST UNS ERFREUEN, LM with refrain – *All Creatures Of Our God And King*, 78 – *God Our Refuge*, 80   ↓_↓↓ ↓_
open C   C Am G7   C Am G7   Am↓↓ F G7   Am G7 C   Am G7 C   tr i m tr i m
REFRAIN   F↓↓ G7 C   Am↓↓ F G7   F↓↓ G7 C   Am   A E C A E G

LAUDA ANIMA 87 87 87 – *Praise My Soul The King Of Heaven*, 121   ↓↑_↑
open G   G7 • C Am   F Am F Dm   E7 • Am G7   G6 E7 C G7   r m i t
          C Am C Am   • F G7 C ↓   A G E C

LET US BREAK BREAD 10 10 with refrain – *Let Us Break Bread Together*, 143   ↓↑↓↑
open G (low)   _C G7 C Am   G7 F G7 C   G7 • F Dm   Am F C ↓   r m i t   A G E C

CHORD PROGRESSIONS
149

LLANFAIR 77 77 – *Christ The Lord Is Ris'n Today*, 61   ↑_↑↓
     open C   **C Am G7 Dm**   **G7 Am Dm C**   **C Am G7 Dm**   **G7 Am Dm C**   *tr m i m*
     E7 G7 F Dm   **C • G7 •**   **C Am G7 Dm**   **G7 Am Dm C**   A G E C

LOBE DEN HERREN 14 14 4 7 8 – *Praise To The Lord the Almighty*, 123   ↓↑↓
     open C   **C E7 Am F Dm G7 C ↓**   **• E7 Am F Dm G7 C ↓**   *tr m i*
     G7 Am   **C G7 E7 ↓**   **G7 F Dm C ↓**   Claw A ↓ G

LOURDES HYMN 11 11 with refrain – *Immaculate Mary*, 10   ↓_↓↑↓_ or ↓↑↓
     open G (low)   **_C Am G7 C**   **• Am G7 C**   **F C G7 C**   **F C G7 C ↓**   *tr i m*   A E C A E G

LUBECK 77 77 – *On This Day The First Of Days*, 119   ↓_↓↑   *tr m i m*
     open C   **C G7 F C**   **G7 Dm Am G7**   **Am G7 Dm F**   **Am G7 Dm C**   A C E G

MCKEE, CM – *In Christ There Is No East Or West*, 102 – *The King Shall Come*, 16   ↓↑_↑
     – *The Head That Once Was Crowned With Thorns*, 71   *r m i t*
     open C   **_C G7 C7 F**   **Am F C**   **Am**   **E7 C G6 C**   **E7 G7 C**   **G7**   A C E G

MENDELSSOHN 7777777777 – *Hark The Herald Angels Sing*, 23   ↓↑↓↑
     open G (low)   **C F C Am**   **G7 • E7 C**   **• F C Am**   **G7 F G7 •**   *tr m i m*
     C • F Am   **C • F Am**   **F •↓↑ C↓↑ F↓↑ Am↓↑ F**   **G7 C F C**   A C E G
     REFRAIN   **F •↓↑ C↓↑ F↓↑ Am↓↑ F**   **G7 C F C ↓**

MUELLER 11 11 11 11 – *Away In A Manger*, 18   ↓_↓↑↓_ or ↓↑↓   *m r i t* or *t m i r m i*
     open G   **_C Am F C**   **G7 • C Am**   **C Am F C**   **G7 C G7 C ↓**   A E C A E G

NEW BRITAIN, CM – *Amazing Grace*, 77   ↓_↓↑↓_ or ↓↑↓   *tr i m*
     open G (low)   **_C C7 F C**   **• Am G7 ↓**   **C C7 F C**   **Am G6 C ↓**   A E C A E G   Claw A ↓ G

NICAEA 11 12 12 10 – *Holy Holy Holy*, 97   ↓_↓↑   *tr m i m*
     open C   **C Am G7 •**   **F • C G6**   **G7 • C G6**   **G7 Dm G7 •**
     C Am G7 •   **F • G7 •**   **C G7 F Am F G7 C •**   A C E G

NUN DANKET 67 67 66 66 – *Now Thank We All Our God*, 111   ↓_↓↑   *tr m i m*
     open G   **_G7 F G7 •**   **F G7 Dm C G6**   **G7 F G7 •**   **F G7 Dm C G7**
     • C G7 •   **C F G7 •**   **F Dm F •**   **Dm F C •**   A C E G

O DU FROLICHE 55 7 55 7 – *O Sanctissima*, 138   ↓↑↓   *tr i m*
     open G   **C F G7 Am F ↓**   **C F G7 Am F ↓**   **C • F G7 E7 Am C ↓**
     G6 G7 F Dm   **E7 G7 C G7**   **F Am F C E7 G7 C ↓**   A E C A E G

O FILII ET FILIAE 888 – *Ye Sons And Daughters*, 73 – *Lord God Sabaoth El Adonai*, 142   ↓_↓↑↓_   *tr m i*
     open A (low)   **F C G7 F**   **• C G7 F**   **• Am C E7**   **G7 Am**   **Am F C E7 G7 Am ↓**   A E C A E G

O Holy Night, 29   ↓↑↓
     open E   **C • G7 • F C G7**   **C • • G7 F C •**   **• • G7 • F • C G7**   **• E7 • G7 F E7 • • •**
     G7 • • • F C Am G7   **• F G7 • F C G7**   **Am • • E7 • • • G7 Dm • • • Am • • •**
     C • G7 • F • • • C • G7 F C • • •   **G7 • • C E7↓ X X X**   **E7 G7 C ↓**

O WALY WALY, LM – *How Lovely Is Your Dwelling Place*, 99   ↓_↓↑↓_
     open G (low)   **_C Am F C**   **Am F C G7**   **Am G7 F C**   **F G7 F C**   *tr m i*   A E C A E G

OLD HUNDREDTH, LM – *Praise God From Whom All Blessings Flow*, 120 – *The Word Of God Proceeded Forth*, 58   ↓_↓↑
     open C   **_C Am F E7**   **C Am F G7**   **G6 E7 Am C**   **Am F G6 C ↓**   *r m i t*   A C E G

PASSION CHORALE 76 76 D – *O Sacred Head Now Wounded*, 50 – *O Sacred Head Surrounded*, 51   ↓↑_↑
     open E   **_F Dm G7 C**   **• E7 F ↓**   **• Dm G7 C**   **• E7 F ↓**   *m r i t i t*
     G7 F C •   **F Dm E7 ↓**   **G7 C Am E7**   **Dm G7 C ↓**   A C E G

150 CHORD PROGRESSIONS

PICARDY 87 87 87 - *Let All Mortal Flesh Keep Silence, 91* – *Face To Face, 90* - *Stephen Deacon Proto-Martyr, 140*   ↓↑↓↑
   open A (low)   F C Am • G6 •   Am F Dm Am C •   F C Am • G6 •   Am F Dm Am C •   r m i t
                    Am F G7 • Am ↓↑ C G7 •   C F G7 E7 Am •   A G E C

PLEADING SAVIOR 87 87 D (*Sing of Mary Pure and Lowly*) – *Hark A Thrilling Voice Is Sounding, 22*
    – *Praise the Lord You Heav'ns Adore, 122* – *Holy Mary Graceful Mother, 136* – *Holy Joseph, 137*   ↓↑_↑
   open E   C F C G6 C F G6 C   • F C G6 C F G6 C   r m i t
              G6 G7 F Am G6 G7 F G7   C F C Am C F E7 C   A G E C

PUER NOBIS NASCITUR, LM – *Full Easter Joy The Day Was Bright, 63*   ↓↑↓ tr m i
   open G (low)   _C Am • C   G7 • C •   F G7 Am G7   C G7 Am C   A E C A E G Claw A↓G

Rise Up Shepherd And Follow, 32   ↓↑ ↓↑
   3rd fret A   _C • G7 C   G7 C7 F C↓   • • G7 C   • G7 F C↓   r m i t
       REFRAIN   • • G7 •   • C7 F C↓   • G7 F Am   C G7 F C↓   A C E G

SALZBURG 77 77 D – *Songs Of Thankfulness And Praise, 38* – *At The Lamb's High Feast We Sing, 64*   ↓_↓
    – *Holy Feast You Holy Day, 65* (for Easter), *66* (for Ascension), *67* (for Pentecost)   or ↑_↑↓
   open G   C G7 •   G7 F Dm C   • G7 • C   G7 F Dm C   r m i t
            G7 G6 C G7   F C E7 Am   C F C G7   Am F G7 C   A G E C

SINE NOMINE 10 10 10 with alleluias – *For All The Saints, 141*   ↓_↓↑ r m i t
   open G   _C F C   G7 E7 F G7   C G7 Dm G7   F C G7 C   A G E C A G E C

Somebody's Knockin', 54   ↓↑↓↑
   open C   C F C •   G7 F G7 •   • F Am C   • F C •   t i m r
       VERSE   • •   • F C •   G7 •   REFRAIN   • F G7 •   • F Am C   • F C •   A C E G

ST AGNES, 86 86 CM – *Shepherd of Souls, 124* – *We Walk By Faith, 125*   ↑_↑↓↑_ or ↓↑↓
   open E   C G7 F C   G7 C G7   Dm G7 E7 C   G7 Am C Am   tr m i A E C A E G

ST ANNE, 86 86 CM – *O God Our Help In Ages Past, 115*   ↓↑_↑
   open C   _F C F Dm   F Dm C G7   F G7 F E7   Dm G6 F   C   tr m i m A C E G

ST CATHERINE, LM – *Faith Of Our Ancestors, 7*   ↓_↓↑↓_
   open E   C Am G7 C   • Am F G7   E7 Am G7 C   • C7 G7 C   tr m i
            F C E7 C   • F G7 C ↓   A E C A E G

ST COLUMBA, 86 86 CM – *O Breathe On Me O Breath Of God, 116* – *The King of Love My Shepherd Is, 117*   ↓_↓↑↓_
   open C   _Am G7 Am C   Am G7 C C7   F G7 C Am   G7 Am C •   tr m i tr m i A E C A E G

ST DENIO 11 11 11 11 – *Eternal Invisible God Only Wise, 83* – *At Break Of Day, 82*   ↓_↓↓_
   open C   _F G7 C Am   F G7 C Am   C G6 C E7   F G7 E7 C C7   tr i m A E C A E G

ST ELIZABETH – *Beautiful Savior, 86*   ↓↑_↑
   open C   C • G7 C   Am • F C   G7 F G7 F   Dm Am E7 G7   r m i t
            C Dm G7 F   • G7 F C   E7 G7 Am G7 C ↓   A G E C

ST FLAVIAN, CM – *Lord Who Throughout These Forty Days, 48*   ↓↑_↑
   open C   _C F G7 C   F G7 E7 Am   • G7 C E7   G7 F C ↓   r m i t A C E G

ST LOUIS 86 86 76 86 – *O Little Town Of Bethlehem, 30*   ↓_↓↑
   open E   _C • G7 F   C G7 E7 •   • Am G7 F   C E7 C •   tr m i m
            Am E7 G7 •   F Am E7 G7   C Am G7 F   G7 E7 C ↓   A C E G

ST THEODULPH, 76 76 D – *All Glory Laud And Honor, 42*   ↓↑_↑
   open G (low)   _C G7 F • C F • Am   C G7 F • C Am F Am   tr m i m
            F C E7 Am F G7 C C7   Am G7 C Am C7 G7 F ↓   A C E G

ST THOMAS 87 87 87 (*Tantum Ergo*) – *Sing My Tongue The Savior's Glory, 53* – *In His Temple come Behold Him, 24*
   open C   C Am F Dm C   Am Dm G7 C   • • F Dm C   ↓_↓↑
            Am C Am G7   • C G7 Dm C   F Dm G7 C ↓   r m i t A C E G

CHORD PROGRESSIONS

ST THOMAS 66 86 (Williams) – *The Advent Of Our King*, 15   ↓↑_↑
open G (low)   _ C Am G7 ↓   C F G7 ↓   C G7 C G7 F G7 C ↓   *tr m i m*   A C E G

STABAT MATER 88 7 – *Virgin-Born We Bow Before You*, 37 – *At The Cross Her Station Keeping*, 59   ↓_↓↑
open C   C Am • F C↓   • Am F Am G7↓   • E7 G7 C↓   *r m i t*   A C E G

STILLE NACHT – *Silent Night*, 33   ↓↑↓   *tr i m*
2nd fret C   G • • • D • G •   C • G •   C • G •   D D7 G •   • D7 G   A E C A E G

STUTTGART 87 87 D – *Come Thou Long Expected Jesus*, 4   ↓_↓↑
open G (low)   C Am G7 C   G7 Am G7 C   Am G7 F Am   C G7 F C ↓   *tr m i m*   A C E G

SWEET SACRAMENT, LM – *Jesus My Lord My God My All*, 104   ↓_↓↑↓_
open G   C Am G7 F   Am F G7 C   • Am G7 F   Am F G7 C   *tr m i*
       G7 F G7 C   G7 F G7 F   Am F G7 C   A E C A E G

TALLIS CANON, LM – *Take Lord Receive* (*O God Grant Me Serenity*), 130   ↓↑↓   *m r i t   m r i t*
open C   _ C Am G7 Am   F C G7 C   F C G7 C   F C G7 C • • •   A E C A E G   Claw A↓G

THE CALL 7777 – *Singular Justice* (*Of Your Singular Justice We Sing*), 129   ↓↑↓
open C   C Em Am G7   C Em Am G7   C7 Am C G7   *tr m i*   or   *r m i t   i t*
       F Am G6↓↑ F↓↑ G7↓↑ E7 C •   A E C A E G   or   Claw A↓G

The First Noel, 34   ↓_↓↑↓_
open E   C G7 C G7   C G7 C E7   C G7 C G7   C G7 C E7   *tr m i*
REFRAIN   C G7 F C   F C F C ↓   A E C A E G

The Lord's Prayer, 145   C G7 F C G7 E7   F G7 F G7 G6 G7 • C   ↓↑↓↑ or ↓ (with thumb)
open E   F G7 E7 G7 C F C •   • C7 F G7 •   *tr m i m*
       F Am G7 •   F G7 C •   Am • C •   G C E A

UNDE ET MEMORES 10 10 10 10 10 10 – *Lord When At Your Last Supper*, 106 – *Draw Near To Your Jerusalem O Lord*, 8
         – *The Angel Gabriel From Heaven Came*, 9 – *Open The Portals*, 107   ↓↑_↑
open E   _ C F Am C G7 •   • F Am C E7 •   C F Am C G6 •   *r m i t*
       Am • G7 E7 G7 •   C F Am C G7 •   F Am C G7 C •   A C E G

VENEZ DIVIN MESSIE 78 76 – *O Come Divine Messiah*, 11   ↓↑↓
open G (low)   _ C Am F C   F Am C G7   C Am F C   Am G7 C ↓   *tr i m*
REFRAIN   G7 Am C •   G7 Am C •   F G7 F G7   F G7 E7 G7 ↓   Claw A ↓ G

VENI CREATOR SPIRITUS, LM – *Come Creator Spirit*, 74   ↓↑↓   *tr m i*   A C E G
open C   _ C Dm F •   • Dm G7 •   F Am C Dm •   G7 C7 G7 C • ↓   A E C A E G

VENI EMMANUEL, LM – *O Come O Come Emmanuel*, 12 – *Let Glory Be To God On High*, 105   ↓↑_↑ ↓↑_↑
open A (low)   _ Am G7 Am   C G7 Am   F C G7   Am G7 Am   *tr m i m tr m i m*
REFRAIN   G7 Am G7 Am   C E7 Am ↓   A C E G A C E G

VICTORY 888 with alleluias – *The Strife Is O'er*, 72   ↓↑↓
open G   C F G7 C   E7 Am F G7   C F G7 C   • G7 C ↓   *tr i m*
       • G7 C ↓   G7 F G7 ↓   G6 E7 C ↓   A E C A E G   or   Claw A↓G

WERNER (O Salutaris Hostia) – *O Saving Victim*, 49   ↓↑↓ or ↓_↓
open G (low)   C F Dm C   • G7 F C   • Am F G7   C Am E7 C   *tr m i*   A G E C

WINCHESTER NEW, CM – *On Jordan's Bank*, 14   ↓↑_↑
open C   _ F Dm C Am   C7 G7 C •   F Dm C7 G7   F C F •   *tr m i m*   A C E G

WONDROUS LOVE 12 9 12 12 9 – *What Wondrous Love Is This*, 134   ↓↑↓↑   *r m i t*
2nd fret C   _ G7 F G7 E7   C F G7 ↓   F G7 C G7   E7 F G7 C   Am F G7 ↓   A C E G A C E G

INDEX of MELODIES

ADESTE FIDELIS – *O Come All Ye Faithful*, 27
ADORE TE DEVOTE 11 11 11 11 – *At The Name of Jesus*, 43 – *O My God My God Why*, 44
AMERICA 66 4 666 4 – *America (My Country 'tis of Thee)*, 144
ANTIOCH, CM – *Joy To The World*, 26
AURELIA 76 76 D – *The Church's One Foundation*, 126 – *The Day Of Resurrection*, 70
    – *Our Father All Creating*, 127 – *We Plow The Fields And Scatter*, 128

BEAUTIFUL MOTHER 77 77 – *On This Day O Beautiful Mother*, 139
BUNESSAN 5554 D (Morning Has Broken) – *As Abba Loves You*, 81

CAROL, CMD – *It Came Upon The Midnight Clear*, 25
CONDITOR, LM – *Creator Of The Stars Of Night*, 6

DIADEMATA – *Crown Him With Many Crowns*, 46 (for Lent), 62 (for Easter), 89 (for Ordinary Time)
DIVINUM MYSTERIUM 87 87 87 7 – *Of The Father's Love Begotten*, 31
DIX 77 77 77 – *For The Beauty Of The Earth*, 94 – *Glady Magi From Of Old*, 19
DUKE STREET, LM – *From All That Dwell Below The Skies*, 92 – *I Know That My Redeemer Lives*, 93

EASTER HYMN 77 77 with alleluias – *Jesus Christ Is Ris'n Today*, 68
EIN' FESTE BURG 87 87 66 66 7 – *A Mighty Fortress Is Our God*, 76
ELLACOMBE 76 76 D – *I Sing The Mighty Pow'r Of God*, 101
ENDLESS SONG 87 87 – *How Can I Keep From Singing*, 98
ERHALT UNS HERR, LM – *The Glory Of These Forty Days*, 56 – *Take Up Your Cross*, 57
    – *The God Whom Earth And Sea And Sky*, 36
ES IST EIN' ROS' ENTSPRUNGEN 76 76 6 76 – *Lo, How a Rose E'er Blooming*, 41

FESTIVAL CANTICLE – *Great Are The Works of the Lord*, 95
FINLANDIA 10 10 10 10 10 10 – *Be Still My Soul*, 135
FOREST GREEN 86 86 86 86 – *O Lord Of Life*, 118
FRIEND – *What A Friend We Have In Jesus*, 133

GENEVA 42 87 87 77 88 – *Comfort Comfort O My People*, 5, 88
GLORIA 77 77 with refrain – *Angels We Have Heard On High*, 17
Go Tell It On The Mountain, 20
GOD REST YOU MERRY 86 86 86 with refrain – *God Rest Ye Merry Gentle Folk*, 21
GREENSLEEVES 87 87 with refrain – *What Child Is This*, 40
GROSSER GOTT 78 78 77 – *Holy God We Praise Your Name*, 96

HAMBURG – *When I Survey The Wondrous Cross*, 55
HEINLEIN 7 7 7 7 – *Forty Days and Forty Nights*, 47 – *Come Redeemer Of Our Race*, 3
HYFRYDOL 87 87 D – *Alleluia! Sing To Jesus*, 60 – *Love Divine All Love Excelling*, 112
    – *Prophets Out of Ancient Times*, 113 – *There's A Wideness In God's Mercy*, 114
HYMN TO JOY 8787D – *Joyful Joyful We Adore You*, 85 – *Blessed Be*, 84 – *Sing With All The Saints In Glory*, 69

IHR KINDERLEIN KOMMET 11 11 11 11 – *O Come Little Children*, 28
ITALIAN HYMN (MOSCOW) 664 6664 – *Lord Your Almighty Word (Let There Be Light)*, 110

JESU DULCIS MEMORIA, LM (O Radiant Light O Sun Divine) – *Lord Of All Being Throned Afar*, 108
    – *To You We Owe Our Hymn of Praise*, 109 – *Blest Holy (The Beatitudes)*, 131

KINGS OF ORIENT 88 44 6 with refrain – *We Three Kings Of Orient Are*, 39
KINGSFOLD, CMD – *I Heard The Voice Of Jesus Say*, 100 – *Praise To The Holiest In The Height*, 52
KREMSER 12 11 12 11 – *We Gather Together*, 132

LAMBILLOTTE, LM – *Come Holy Spirit Whoever One*, 87
LAND OF REST 86 86 CM – *Jerusalem My Happy Home*, 103
LASST UNS ERFREUEN, LM with refrain – *All Creatures Of Our God And King*, 78 – *God Our Refuge*, 80
LAUDA ANIMA 87 87 87 – *Praise My Soul The King Of Heaven*, 121
LET US BREAK BREAD 10 10 with refrain – *Let Us Break Bread Together*, 143
LLANFAIR 77 77 – *Christ The Lord Is Ris'n Today*, 61
LOBE DEN HERREN 14 14 4 7 8 – *Praise To The Lord the Almighty*, 123

INDEX of MELODIES

LOURDES HYMN 11 11 with refrain – *Immaculate Mary*, 10
LUBECK 77 77 – *On This Day The First Of Days*, 119

MCKEE, CM – *In Christ There Is No East Or West*, 102 – *The King Shall Come*, 16
    – *The Head That Once Was Crowned With Thorns*, 71
MENDELSSOHN 7777777777 – *Hark The Herald Angels Sing*, 23
MUELLER 11 11 11 11 – *Away In A Manger*, 18

NEW BRITAIN, CM – *Amazing Grace*, 77
NICAEA 11 12 12 10 – *Holy Holy Holy*, 97
NUN DANKET 67 67 66 66 – *Now Thank We All Our God*, 111

O DU FROLICHE 55 7 55 7 – *O Sanctissima*, 138
O FILII ET FILIAE 888 – *Ye Sons And Daughters*, 73 – *Lord God Sabaoth El Adonai*, 142
O Holy Night, 29
O WALY WALY, LM – *How Lovely Is Your Dwelling Place*, 99
OLD HUNDREDTH, LM – *Praise God From Whom All Blessings Flow*, 120 – *The Word Of God Proceeded Forth*, 58

PASSION CHORALE 76 76 D – *O Sacred Head Now Wounded*, 50 – *O Sacred Head Surrounded*, 51
PICARDY 87 87 87 - *Let All Mortal Flesh Keep Silence*, 91 – *Face To Face*, 90 - *Stephen Deacon Proto-Martyr*, 140
PLEADING SAVIOR 87 87 D (Sing of Mary Pure and Lowly) – *Hark A Thrilling Voice Is Sounding*, 22
    – *Praise the Lord You Heav'ns Adore*, 122 – *Holy Mary Graceful Mother*, 136 – *Holy Joseph*, 137
PUER NOBIS NASCITUR, LM – *Full Easter Joy The Day Was Bright*, 63

Rise Up Shepherd And Follow, 32

SALZBURG 77 77 D – *Songs Of Thankfulness And Praise*, 38 – *At The Lamb's High Feast We Sing*, 64
    – *Holy Feast You Holy Day*, 65 (for Easter), 66 (for Ascension), 67 (for Pentecost)
SINE NOMINE 10 10 10 with alleluias – *For All The Saints*, 141
Somebody's Knockin', 54
ST AGNES, 86 86 CM – *Shepherd of Souls*, 124 – *We Walk By Faith*, 125
ST ANNE, 86 86 CM – *O God Our Help In Ages Past*, 115
ST CATHERINE, LM – *Faith Of Our Ancestors*, 7
ST COLUMBA, 86 86 CM – *O Breathe On Me O Breath Of God*, 116 – *The King of Love My Shepherd Is*, 117
ST DENIO 11 11 11 11 – *Eternal Invisible God Only Wise*, 83 – *At Break Of Day*, 82
ST ELIZABETH – *Beautiful Savior*, 86
ST FLAVIAN, CM – *Lord Who Throughout These Forty Days*, 48
ST LOUIS 86 86 76 86 – *O Little Town Of Bethlehem*, 30
ST THEODULPH, 76 76 D – *All Glory Laud And Honor*, 42
ST THOMAS 87 87 87 (Tantum Ergo) – *Sing My Tongue The Savior's Glory*, 53 – *In His Temple come Behold Him*, 24
ST THOMAS 66 86 (Williams) – *The Advent Of Our King*, 15
STABAT MATER 88 7 – *Virgin-Born We Bow Before You*, 37 – *At The Cross Her Station Keeping*, 59
STILLE NACHT – *Silent Night*, 33
STUTTGART 87 87 D – *Come Thou Long Expected Jesus*, 4
SWEET SACRAMENT, LM – *Jesus My Lord My God My All*, 104

TALLIS CANON, LM – *Take Lord Receive (O God Grant Me Serenity)*, 130
THE CALL 7777 – *Singular Justice (Of Your Singular Justice We Sing)*, 129
The First Noel, 34
The Lord's Prayer, 145

UNDE ET MEMORES 10 10 10 10 10 10 – *Lord When At Your Last Supper*, 106 – *Open The Portals*, 107
    – *Draw Near To Your Jerusalem O Lord*, 8 – *The Angel Gabriel From Heaven Came*, 9

VENEZ DIVIN MESSIE 78 76 – *O Come Divine Messiah*, 11
VENI CREATOR SPIRITUS, LM – *Come Creator Spirit*, 74
VENI EMMANUEL, LM – *O Come O Come Emmanuel*, 12 – *Let Glory Be To God On High*, 105
VICTORY 888 with alleluias – *The Strife Is O'er*, 72

WERNER (O Salutaris Hostia) – *O Saving Victim*, 49
WINCHESTER NEW, CM – *On Jordan's Bank*, 14
WONDROUS LOVE 12 9 12 12 9 – *What Wondrous Love Is This*, 134

www.ingramcontent.com/pod-product-compliance
Lightning Source LLC
Chambersburg PA
CBHW081350080526
44588CB00016B/2435